Maggie's Table

Maggie Beer

Photography by Simon Griffiths

VIKING

Viking
Penguin Books Australia Ltd
487 Maroondah Highway, PO Box 257
Ringwood, Victoria 3134, Australia
Penguin Books Ltd
Harmondsworth, Middlesex, England
Penguin Putnam Inc.
375 Hudson Street, New York
New York 10014, USA
Penguin Books Canada Limited
10 Alcorn Avenue, Toronto, Ontario
Canada M4V 3B2
Penguin Books (N.Z.) Ltd
Cnr Rosedale and Airborne Roads
Albany, Auckland, New Zealand
Penguin Books (South Africa) (Pty) Ltd
5 Watkins Street, Denver Ext 4, 2094
South Africa
Penguin Books India (P) Ltd
11, Community Centre, Panchsheel Park
New Delhi 110 017, India

First published by
Penguin Books Australia Ltd 2001

10 9 8 7 6 5 4 3 2 1

Designed by Sandy Cull, Penguin Design Studio
Photography by Simon Griffiths
Scarecrow photographs on pages 60–1 by Eric Algra
Typeset in Trade Gothic by J&M Typesetting
Printed in China by Midas Printing (Asia) Ltd

National Library of Australia
Cataloguing-in-Publication data:

  Beer, Maggie.
  Maggie's table.

  Includes index.
  ISBN 0 670 889792.

  1. Cookery, Australian. I. Griffiths, Simon
  (Simon John). II. Title.

641.5994

Also by Maggie Beer

Maggie's Farm

Maggie's Orchard

Stephanie Alexander & Maggie Beer's Tuscan Cookbook (co-author)

Cooking with Verjuice

www.penguin.com.au

For Zöe, Max and Lily, who I feel will always share my love of the Barossa and our home

Contents

Introduction   It was the luckiest accident of my life that Colin and I settled in South Australia's Barossa Valley. If I believed in such things, I might say that fate had a hand in it all: it has always felt that it was just meant to be. Whatever the reason, the quality of our life here is so deep and rich, and so centred around the soil, the seasons and the community, that I now wonder I was ever a city person.

We arrived in the Barossa in the early 1970s after moving from Sydney to 'live in the country' and breed pheasants. The fact that we had also bought a vineyard – not knowing anything about viticulture – in order to provide income until the birds were established is an indication of our youthful idealism! Our site selection was equally romantic: we had chosen the Valley simply for its aesthetics as we loved the fresh, green landscape of vines we drove through en route from Sydney to Col's family at Mallala.

What makes the Barossa so very special is that the early European settlers, German-speaking Silesians who arrived in the Valley from as early as 1841, brought with them a strong food culture, a love of music and deep religious convictions that still allowed them to express those aspects of their heritage freely. These people were small farmers, in the Australian scheme of things; they tended to be self-sufficient, they married their familiar foods to the new climate and conditions, and their food was intimately linked to their seasonal celebrations, many of which still exist today. In my view, the fact that the food heritage of those early settlers is the closest thing we could have to a peasant culture in Australia is the Valley's main and continuing strength.

The Lutheran ethic still runs deep today, and the many beautiful churches that dot the Valley are constant reminders of our past. But at a more basic level, it's the butchers and bakers who, to me, keep alive the ideals of those early men and women. Lachsschinken, mettwurst, streuselkuchen and bienenstich are everyday items to people in the Barossa, yet they epitomise what is different about this very special valley to anyone visiting.

The Barossa is surely one of the world's greatest trademarks. No matter where I am, I need only mention I'm from the Valley and there is immediate recognition thanks to our legendary wine industry, our famous hospitality and now our small but internationally recognised Barossa Music Festival. The Barossa has a cachet I know others envy, but it's not something that can be replicated easily. This love of food, wine and music, and the community's willingness and ability to pull together as a whole, are so entrenched they are now recognised as being part of the Barossa ethic. It's so rare to see competing businesses working with each other to help support their area as we in the Barossa do, not only during our festivals but at any time we're showing the Valley to the world. I can't tell you how proud I am to be able to say I'm from the Barossa.

Living in the Valley has certainly taught and given me a great deal. Born into a family where food was always important, I guess my eyes and ears were wide open when I first arrived here. I learnt quickly about the rhythm of the seasons, how to delight in fruit and vegetables picked ripe and at their best, and how to maximise the potential of not only what can be grown here but what is available in the wild. To share in a community as a city person was particularly special, but to find myself in a place so devoted to my own passions – food, music and wine – made it seem, soon after arriving, that it was meant to be.

The whole idea of farming pheasants was a pretty wild idea, given that most of the population wasn't familiar with game birds when we started. But in 1977 Col was awarded a Churchill Fellowship to tour Europe and America and study the rearing of game birds. Within months of our return from that tour, we opened a farm shop to sell our produce direct to the public, as we'd seen done in Scotland. Shortly after that the shop became the Pheasant Farm Restaurant, which showcased Barossa produce and was to dominate our lives until 1993. None of this, nor our subsequent expansion into the export market with our range of food products, would have been possible had it not been for the food culture and work ethic that permeate the Valley, or the marvellous support networks that run through the community.

Creating a sense of place and permanence is as much a part of the Barossa make-up as is the willingness to have a go, and another legacy of those early settlers. By the mid-1980s, living and working at the Pheasant Farm was taking its toll. And then, on a weekly horse ride with friends, I saw a tall old German-style cottage set on the side of a hill near Tanunda. This became the ride I'd urge the others to take – the road was so steep we used to let fly and gallop up the hill to gather our breath at the top, overlooking the valley. I don't know how many times I rode past this cottage before I stopped to ask the owners if they had ever considered selling. From astride my horse I could see a dam at the bottom of the garden surrounded by mature willows and gums, and three huge pear trees. The farm sheds mirrored the design of the high-roofed cottage – all unspoilt and very beautiful. The rest, as they say, is history: two years later we bought the cottage and its surrounding 9 hectares.

Having an orchard had been the dream of my country life, but the poor soil and lack of water at the Pheasant Farm had made it impossible to grow anything but quinces, olives or grapevines.

The soil on the cottage block was deep, sandy loam and we now had the luxury of mains water – finally I could have my orchard. Was this another case of 'this was just meant to be'? Even though I thought it unusual that the cottage didn't have its own orchard, I realise that starting from scratch was even better, as it gave me the freedom to choose the varieties I most coveted. Both the orchard and kitchen garden are pretty close now to what I originally imagined, and they have provided a balance to our life here and to my cooking. There is nothing more engaging for a cook than to work closely with the freshest of fresh produce. I love wandering out in the early morning to choose fruit for breakfast or to walk through the orchard on a summer's evening, when the scent of the fruit declares its ripeness, to pick asparagus or artichokes that will go into the pot within minutes. This is such a luxury in these busy times, whereas it would simply have been an everyday part of life for the Barossa's early settlers.

This book, then, is a celebration of the life I share with Colin, our family and our friends in the Barossa. It is a celebration of home, a region and its seasons, farmers and their produce, traditional bakers and butchers who enjoy new challenges, and it is about community.

And the essence of that life is sharing our table. I love to cook, whether it's with our little grandchildren at the end of a frantic week, or for a midweek meal with Col, a supper after a concert or a feast for a crowd of friends. 'Going with the flow' has become my catchcry, and simplicity the key. With two passionate cooks in the family (our elder daughter, Saskia, is the other, while her sister, Ellie, has a great palate), there are lots of 'I'll bring this' and 'You do that'. We love cooking and eating outside whatever the season, and over the years our food has got simpler and simpler, involving everyone as much as possible.

This book is my way of saying thank you to the Barossa for welcoming me so warmly all those years ago, and for giving us the freedom to realise our dreams. I invite you now to join my family and me at our table.

summerautumnwinterspring

A Feast for Sixty   As much as I love the excitement of travel, home in the Barossa is my life. After a hectic year 2000, which meant that I'd frequently been away from my family and we'd seen little of our friends, we decided to have a pre-Christmas party to celebrate all the things we enjoy about being at home. I love any excuse for gathering people I like together, but this time I had two extra reasons: our new room or 'pavilion' and the wood-fired oven in our court-yard were finally finished. A sheet of paper and a pen and suddenly we were having sixty to lunch!

The fact that the date we chose was only a week after returning from a confer-ence in Europe made things a bit more frenetic than usual, but as I believe in serving simple food, that's exactly what we ended up doing, which helped. That doesn't mean everything ran to plan. Nothing much I do actually does, but I've become pretty good at going with the flow.

Cooking yabbies from our own dam for parties was the first family tradition we

established after moving into the cottage in 1987 on our elder daughter Saskia's fourteenth birthday (Ellie, our other daughter, was twelve). Planning our summer party while still overseas, I just assumed that we'd be able to follow tradition – but we'd had no late spring rains to fill the dam, which meant no yabbies. Thankfully I was able to persuade a local yabby farmer to drain his own dams for me. Yet another friend lent us a turbo-charged crab cooker on which we sat the 40-litre pot we keep for cooking yabbies on such occasions. The way people put themselves out to find solutions to problems is one of the great things about life in the Barossa.

On the morning of the party Colin was up at 5 a.m. to light the wood oven. We'd only had one trial run before the day of the feast and were armed with so many instructions that the task ahead was suddenly a little daunting, but we were willing to take the chance. Simplicity was the key, and we'd planned to do masses of Barossa chook thighs with preserved lemon and potatoes (page 54) as our main dish, with roasted waxy potatoes and pancetta as an extra (page 28). I have to admit to a bit of trickery in the end as the oven ranged from not hot enough to absolutely raging, so there was a lot of to-ing and fro-ing between it and the traditional ovens in the kitchen!

None of this mattered in the end. The day was so festive – the weather was warm without being too hot, our friends arrived well hatted and in bright colours, and the music, always loud and often operatic, added to the general din in the best way. Everyone grabbed whatever chairs were to hand and sat under market umbrellas or, as so often happens here, just propped themselves on the many steps at the rear of the cottage. The cooking of the yabbies provided early entertainment, and a throng gathered around Col as he fished the freshly boiled yabbies from the pot set up under our huge pear tree on the side of the dam. Our old iron washstands stood at the ready as communal fingerbowls and my favourite tea towels were put to good use dealing with wet hands.

Our courtyard and the new wood oven drew the curious, glass in hand, who were enthusiastic about the idea of putting one in themselves (until they heard how early Col had to get up). Then there were those who moved, as they always do, into the kitchen, the centre of our home, whether it was to help or just talk.

The pavilion provided yet another eating area. This new, airy and beautifully peaceful room, almost all glass with a soaring timber ceiling, is connected to our 1860s stone cottage by a glass walkway. It has brought the house even closer to our dam and pool, making the transition from inside to outside almost seamless. This is where I keep my piano, and occasionally a friend was tempted to play in a style much grander than my own.

I wandered from group to group, passing pâté and other goodies around, enjoying the chance to relax and chat at leisure, and basking in that wonderful feeling of *bonhomie*. Our eldest grandchildren, Zöe and Max, ran through the crowd, while Lily, just nine months old, was passed to anyone keen for a cuddle. As the day wore on, quiet groups sought the shade of our huge wisteria, where a wooden table is fashioned around the massive trunk and the blossoms gently scent the air.

The party came together beautifully, and we finished the meal with sparkling shiraz jelly heavily set with berries (page 78). It was well into the evening when the last guests left, and I sat too tired to move but happy in the knowledge that our life in the Barossa is extraordinarily rich.

Pickled Plums

I've always loved pickling: I can't bear waste and I love the feeling of plenty that the process produces. But most of all I feel so virtuous when I've finished! Pickled plums go wonderfully with game and offal, particularly Pot-roasted Tongue (page 231).

1 lemon

4 cloves

1 × 2.5 cm piece ginger

600 ml white-wine vinegar

480 g sugar

1 kg blood plums

Remove the zest from the lemon with a potato peeler. Put the zest and all the remaining ingredients except the plums into a large non-reactive saucepan and simmer for 10 minutes, stirring to ensure the sugar has dissolved.

Wash and dry the plums well, then cut them in half and remove the stones. Put the plums into hot, sterilised jars and pour in the hot syrup to cover the fruit, distributing the zest and cloves evenly between the jars as you do so. Allow to cool before sealing, then invert the jars to create a vacuum. Leave for 6 weeks before using. The pickled plums are very firm and wonderful with confit of duck, any poultry terrine or tongue.

Pickled Cherries

If you can't find morello or sour cherries for this recipe, any other cherry will do, but I recommend buying a morello tree from your nursery as they're easy to grow (I have one in my orchard), begin fruiting almost immediately and take this pickle to another dimension. Pickled cherries team best of all with duck or goose, whether they're roasted or made into confit or rillettes.

5 kg sour cherries

2 litres water

3 litres white-wine vinegar

2.5 kg sugar

30 g whole pimento

10 g cloves

20 bay leaves

Wash the cherries, leaving their stems on. Put the water, vinegar, sugar, spices and bay leaves into a large non-reactive pot and stir over gentle heat until the sugar has dissolved, then simmer for 10 minutes. Divide the cherries between hot, sterilised jars, then pour in the hot syrup. Allow to cool before sealing, then invert the jars to create a vacuum. Leave for 6 weeks before using. Try the cherries with cold meats, terrines, pork, duck and the like.

Grape Sauce

Grape sauce is a Barossa institution. My introduction to it was when friends Thea Schubert and Helen Martin made some to sell among the Valley's winemaking fraternity. They packed it into flagons (a mere bottle was never enough) with the year's vintage written on in gold. My version is based on a recipe from another Valley institution, *The Barossa Cookery Book*, first published in 1917.

2 kg very ripe shiraz *or* mataro
  grapes

625 ml white-wine vinegar

600 g Granny Smith apples

1 lemon

3 cloves garlic

400 g sugar

3 teaspoons ground cinnamon

½ teaspoon ground cloves

2 teaspoons cayenne pepper

2 teaspoons sea salt

Put the grapes and vinegar into a large non-reactive pot and squash the grapes with a wooden spoon. Boil over a moderate heat for 1 hour. Put the mixture through a food mill to retrieve as much grape pulp as possible, then discard the pulp and return the sauce to the pot.

Peel, core and grate the apples, then squeeze over lemon juice to prevent discoloration. Finely chop the garlic and put it into the pot with the apple, sugar and spices, then boil vigorously for 20 minutes. Put the sauce through the food mill again, then stir through the salt. Transfer the sauce to hot, sterilised jars or bottles and seal when cool, then invert to create a vacuum. Leave for at least 2 weeks before using. This sauce is traditionally served in the Barossa with sausages or sugar-cured bacon and eggs. I also love it with loin chops.

Homemade Tomato Sauce

I couldn't live without homemade sauce (although I've learnt not to give grandchildren the choice between this and 'shop sauce' as sometimes they forget to give you the right answer!). There's always been the misconception that homemade sauce belongs in the country cook's domain, and that needn't be the case. If you don't have your own tomatoes, a good greengrocer will find what you need.

5 kg vine-ripened tomatoes

1 kg brown onions

3 cloves garlic

125 ml extra-virgin olive oil

3 teaspoons sea salt

2 teaspoons sweet paprika

240 g soft dark-brown sugar

800 ml white-wine vinegar

50 g black peppercorns

30 g cloves

30 g whole allspice

Core and quarter the tomatoes. Peel and roughly chop the onions, and thinly slice the garlic. Put the olive oil into a large non-reactive pot, then add the tomato, onion and garlic and bring to a boil over a high heat. Reduce the heat to moderate, then cook until all the ingredients are very soft.

Stand a food mill over another non-reactive pot and pass the mixture through this to give a semi-smooth pulp (not baby-food smooth). Sprinkle the salt and paprika over the purée, then add the sugar and vinegar and stir to combine. Tie the peppercorns, cloves and allspice up in a small square of muslin or clean Chux, then put this into the pot and bring to a simmer. Simmer gently for several hours until the sauce reaches the desired consistency. Remove the muslin bag and pour the sauce into hot, sterilised bottles. Allow to cool before sealing, then invert to create a vacuum.

Mayonnaise

Homemade mayonnaise is indispensable on my summer table, and making it is a family tradition (there's always a fight to see whose is best). Handmade mayonnaise is silkier than that made in a food processor, and is easy if you have the right bowl. My friend Damien Pignolet has one that is so perfect for the job I've had it copied. The best cooks say a wooden spoon is better than a whisk, too.

2 large free-range egg yolks
  (at room temperature)
1 pinch sea salt
1 teaspoon Dijon mustard
500 ml mellow extra-virgin
  olive oil *or* half extra-virgin
  and half vegetable oil
1 tablespoon verjuice
1 teaspoon finely grated
  lemon zest
squeeze of lemon juice
boiling water

Rinse your chosen bowl with hot water and dry it thoroughly. Whisk or beat the egg yolks with the salt until thick, then add the mustard and whisk until smooth. Continue whisking and add the olive oil drop by drop (until you are a confident mayonnaise-maker, do this painfully slowly!). Once the mixture begins to thicken, you can add the oil in a slow, steady stream, whisking continuously. When the mayonnaise is established, add the verjuice a little at a time, then stir through the zest and juice to taste. Check for seasoning, then add a little boiling water if the mayonnaise needs thinning and requires no more acidulant.

eggs   Don't use too many egg yolks – the flavour can be offputting for some. Two yolks will absorb up to 700 ml olive oil, if you really want to push it.

split mayonnaise   Disaster can be averted if your mayonnaise splits – start again in a clean, dry bowl with a new egg yolk and add the split sauce drop by drop.

flavourings   Once you've mastered a basic mayonnaise, you can use your imagination to change the flavour, texture and colour. Instead of verjuice as the acidulant, try lemon juice or a wine vinegar to suit the dish that will partner the mayonnaise. Raw or roasted garlic can be added, as can anchovies. Make a rouille by blending capsicum purée through aïoli, mayonnaise made with roasted garlic purée. Try adding herbs – basil is wonderful, and lemon thyme mayonnaise is great with snapper. Stir chopped capers, cornichons and parsley through mayonnaise, or take the whole idea a step further and make a rémoulade by starting with hardboiled egg yolks (page 192). For other ideas, look at Sorrel Mayonnaise (page 221) and Crab-mustard Mayonnaise (page 294).

Mushroom and Goat's Cheese Bruschetta

This began as an idea of Stephanie Alexander's for using my mushroom pâté when we were cooking together once for a large group. She pan-fried fresh mushrooms and arranged them like roof tiles on top of toast thickly spread with the pâté. I later added the goat's cheese and finishing touch of the truffle oil to a treat that has since become a regular at our Farm Shop.

unsalted butter

mushrooms

extra-virgin olive oil

marjoram

sea salt

freshly ground black pepper

sliced baguette

goat's cheese

Maggie Beer's Mushroom Pâté

truffle oil

Clarify some butter in a small saucepan by melting it over gentle heat until solids are visible in the bottom of the pan. Strain the butter into a bowl through a very fine sieve to remove the solids, then allow it to firm up in the refrigerator.

Slice the mushrooms fairly thickly and sauté with some butter, a splash of olive oil, a little freshly chopped marjoram, salt and pepper until soft, then remove from the heat.

Preheat the oven to 200°C. Spread the slices of baguette with clarified butter, then bake on baking trays for about 5 minutes or until light golden in colour. Generously spread a layer of goat's cheese over the toast then add another of mushroom pâté, ensuring both are taken right to the edges. Finish by layering the cooked mushrooms on top, one piece slightly overlapping the next, like roof tiles (if your mushrooms are large, just add 1 slice to the bruschetta). Drizzle over a little truffle oil and serve immediately.

mushroom pâté   While I like to think you might use the pâté we make commercially at our farm shop, you can, of course, use your own here.

Olives with Orange, Rosemary and Garlic

I have been so disappointed by the concoctions sold in the name of marinated olives – they are generally in inferior oil, the flavourings are often out of balance and very tired on the palate, and the olives have often been blackened with lye. So I now marinate my own.

250 g cured kalamata olives

1 orange (a Seville orange is
  best of all)

1 teaspoon fresh rosemary
  leaves

1 clove garlic

125 ml extra-virgin olive oil

A few hours before eating, wash the olives well of any brine and dry. Remove the zest from the orange with a potato peeler, being careful to avoid all pith, then slice the zest very finely. Chop the rosemary finely and crush the garlic. Mix all the ingredients and leave to sit at room temperature.

Bruschetta with Tomato and New Season's Extra-virgin Olive Oil

In our house, making bruschettas has become an art form (see opposite). This is Colin's domain and he takes his cue from Aldo Parronchi, a Tuscan friend. The bread must be wood-fired, the fire hot enough to singe the bread, the garlic applied while the toast is hot, and only the freshest extra-virgin olive oil used. Perfect tomatoes, ripe from the vine, are almost reduced to being an added bonus!

green, peppery new season's
  extra-virgin olive oil

sea salt

freshly ground black pepper

thickly sliced wood-fired bread

garlic

small, firm but very ripe vine-
  ripened tomatoes

Preheat the barbecue. Pour a good quantity of olive oil into a large, shallow dish, then season with salt and pepper. Grill the slices of bread, turning when the grill lines appear on the underside (be careful not to blacken the bread too much). Rub cut cloves of garlic over the toasted bread while it is still hot. Encourage your guests to dip the toasted bread into the oil, swishing it around to gather up some salt and pepper too, and to then squeeze a ripe tomato over the bread. Sensational!

Clusters of Roasted Cherry Tomatoes

I've given up picking any small tomatoes I grow and instead dry them at the end of the season or roast them still attached to the vine. The quantities I give here will cover a large platter for a buffet table. Roasted tomatoes of various types usually make their way onto my summer antipasto platters – as shown opposite (I found this exuberant plate while holidaying in Umbria a few years ago).

¼ cup freshly chopped thyme

2 teaspoons sea salt

125 ml extra-virgin olive oil

freshly ground black pepper

2.5 kg cherry *or* small tomatoes
 on the vine

Preheat the oven to 200°C. Mix the thyme and salt into the olive oil, then grind in pepper. Spread the washed and dried tomatoes over 2 baking trays, then drizzle with the seasoned oil, adding more oil if the bases of the trays aren't covered. Roast for 20 minutes if using cherry tomatoes or 5 minutes longer if the tomatoes are slightly larger.

Serve the tomatoes at room temperature as part of a buffet, or with a pot of goat's curd, extra-virgin olive oil, crusty bread or bruschettas and a salad of bitter greens alongside.

slow-cooked tomatoes   Cut 2.5 kg Roma tomatoes in half lengthwise and arrange on baking trays, cut-side up. Sprinkle with 2 tablespoons sea salt and allow to sit for 30 minutes. Drizzle with 2 tablespoons extra-virgin olive oil and bake for 4–5 hours at 120°C until collapsed but still moist. Serve at room temperature, but refrigerate any leftovers as these have a short shelf-life.

oven-roasted tomatoes of indeterminate quality   If you've bought tomatoes of varying degrees of ripeness, let the unripe ones sit at room temperature to achieve the colour they should have been at picking. Throw away any tomatoes that start to rot during this process. Wash 2.5 kg of the survivors and cut them in half lengthwise, then toss with 5 chopped cloves garlic, 2 teaspoons sea salt, 1 tablespoon freshly chopped thyme, 200 ml extra-virgin olive oil and 2 tablespoons sugar (as the tomatoes didn't ripen on the vine, they'll be short on this). Spread the tomatoes out over baking trays and bake for 3½–4½ hours (the cooking time will vary between varieties). Serve at room temperature. If you really want to impress next time you have a party, start with 4 kg!

Eggplant and Caramelised Garlic Salad

The richness of eggplant marries wonderfully with mellow caramelised garlic, underpinned by the gentle acidity of crème fraîche and the freshness of parsley. Perfect as a salad, this combination can also be tossed through hot pasta or served alongside a grilled chop.

12 cloves garlic

extra-virgin olive oil

2 eggplants

flat-leaf parsley

2 handfuls rocket

crème fraîche vinaigrette

¼ cup crème fraîche

¼ cup red-wine vinegar

125 ml extra-virgin olive oil

sea salt

freshly ground black pepper

Bring a small saucepan of water to a boil and blanch the peeled garlic cloves for 5 minutes. Put the garlic into the tiniest saucepan or frying pan you have, then cover with olive oil and cook slowly until caramelised (you can also do this in the oven). Set aside.

Cut the eggplants into 2 cm cubes. In a heavy-based frying pan, pour in olive oil to a depth of 3 cm and heat until very hot. Throw in a piece of bread to test whether the oil is ready – if the bread turns golden brown immediately, the oil is hot enough. Fry a quarter of the eggplant at a time until golden on all sides. Remove from the pan with a slotted spoon to drain on kitchen paper. Cook the remaining eggplant in batches.

To make the vinaigrette, combine the crème fraîche with the vinegar, then add the olive oil, salt and pepper. Combine the warm eggplant and drained garlic cloves in a bowl, then toss with the vinaigrette. Add a generous amount of freshly chopped flat-leaf parsley and check for seasoning. Either serve on a bed of washed and dried rocket, or toss the rocket through the salad at the last minute. **Serves 4**

Christmas Salad

I don't suppose I ever really stint on food, but at Christmas I look even further afield than usual for the most exotic seasonal delicacies. Flavour and balance are my first parameters, but ease of preparation and dramatic effect follow closely behind. This salad easily meets those criteria and has become a firm favourite on our Christmas table.

2 handfuls young rocket

3 witlof bulbs

2 mangoes

1½ ripe avocadoes

¼ papaya

30 mint leaves

lime vinaigrette

2 limes

125 ml extra-virgin olive oil

sea salt

freshly ground black pepper

To make the vinaigrette, finely grate the zest of the limes and juice the fruit, then combine with the olive oil, salt and pepper. Set aside.

Wash and dry the rocket well, and separate the leaves from the witlof. Cut the cheeks from the mangoes and remove the skin. Slice the flesh lengthwise into even strips. Peel the avocadoes and slice them a similar size to the mango strips. Repeat this with the papaya. Finely shred the mint leaves. Toss all the ingredients in a serving bowl with the vinaigrette, then check the seasoning and acidulant. Serve immediately. **Serves 4**

Roasted Waxy Potatoes with Pancetta, Capers and Preserved Lemon

We served this warm 'salad', pictured opposite, at our summer party for sixty (see pages 10–15) with huge success. That day we cooked the potatoes and chook in our wood oven, but it's just as easy to use a domestic one. Wonderful to accompany poultry or grills, this dish is also great for lunch with a green salad.

3 quarters preserved lemon

500 g waxy potatoes (such as
 kipflers)

8 long thin slices pancetta

100 ml extra-virgin olive oil

freshly ground black pepper

1 tablespoon capers

2 tablespoons freshly chopped
 flat-leaf parsley

Preheat the oven to 220°C. Remove the pulp from the preserved lemon and cut the rind into long strips. Wash and dry the potatoes thoroughly, then cut them in half lengthwise. Toss immediately with the preserved lemon, pancetta, olive oil and pepper in a large, shallow, heavy-based baking dish (if the baking dish is too crowded, it's better to divide the potato and so on between 2 dishes so that the potatoes caramelise and the pancetta stays whole and crisp – a crowded pan can mean the contents stew rather than bake). Depending on the oven and the variety of potato used, the cooking time will vary from 20–35 minutes.

Remove the baking dish from the oven and shake to loosen the contents, then add the capers and parsley and check for seasoning. Serve immediately. **Serves 4**

Warm Barossa Potato Salad

This potato salad is a firmly entrenched Barossa dish, although I add the rider to use waxy potatoes. It's always served warm and is a bit of a special-occasion salad as it's quite rich. The traditionally made, sugar-cured bacon is pure Barossa and gives this dish an edge that's impossible to duplicate if mass-produced bacon is used.

1 kg waxy potatoes (such as
 kipfler)

sea salt

1 large red onion

3 rashers sugar-cured bacon

40 g unsalted butter

180 ml cream

2 tablespoons red-wine vinegar

freshly ground black pepper

freshly chopped chives

Wash the potatoes very well, then bring them to a gentle boil in a large saucepan of salted water and cook until just done. (Note that waxy potatoes can take much longer to cook than others, and are better cooked a little more slowly so that their skins don't break.) Drain the potatoes and allow them to cool enough to be handled.

Meanwhile, peel and very finely chop the onion. Crisp the bacon in a dry frying pan. Slip the skins off the potatoes and cut the flesh into cubes. Melt the butter and toss this through the potato in a glass dish with the onion. Cut the bacon into pieces and add it to the potato, then warm the cream and stir it through with the vinegar. Adjust the seasoning and add the chives. Serve while warm. **Serves 4**

Freekah Salad with Preserved Lemon, Quince Paste, Parsley and Mint

Freekah, wheat picked green that's then roasted, is an ancient ingredient from the Middle East. Produced on the Adelaide Plains, Australian freekah can be found in gourmet food stores and good health-food stores, although the bulk of it is exported. I love its nutty flavour – it combines wonderfully with the fresh, sweet–sour and salty flavours in this salad.

400 g freekah (cracked or
   wholegrain) *or* burghul
1.25 litres cold water
sea salt
extra-virgin olive oil
8 quarters preserved lemon
250 g quince paste
2 generous handfuls flat-leaf
   parsley
2 generous handfuls mint
juice of 2 lemons
freshly ground black pepper

Put the freekah, cold water, 1 teaspoon salt and 1 tablespoon olive oil into a large saucepan and bring gently to a boil, stirring occasionally. Cover with a tight-fitting lid, then reduce the temperature and simmer for 10–15 minutes if cooking cracked grain or 25–30 minutes for wholegrain. The water should have been absorbed by the time the freekah is cooked, and the grains should be tender. Tip the freekah into a colander and allow to cool, but don't refrigerate.

Remove the pulp from the preserved lemon and wash the rind, then cut it into tiny dice. Dice the quince paste the same size. Chop the parsley and mint. Toss the cooled freekah with the preserved lemon, quince paste, herbs, lemon juice and 125 ml olive oil, then add pepper and check for salt. Serve, as shown opposite, with Barbecued Quail in a Fig Bath (page 52) or any other grill, or as a side dish to goat's cheese served on a bed of salad leaves. Serves 4

Ricotta and Basil Frittata

To buy a container of fresh ricotta still draining from the night before is the epitome of freshness to me – this is a totally different product from the sealed tubs you see for sale. The combination of good ricotta, our own free-range eggs and basil from the garden means I am more likely to make this frittata than an omelette, particularly as it feeds everyone at once!

375 g wholemilk ricotta

8 large free-range eggs

½ cup freshly grated
  Parmigiano-Reggiano

12 basil leaves

sea salt

freshly ground black

freshly grated nutmeg

1 tablespoon extra-
  olive oil

If the ricotta you have bought doesn't come in a perforated mould through which the whey can ... clean square of muslin or a Chux kitchen cloth. Tie up the corners and hang the ... 30 minutes.

... ggs into a bowl and beat lightly with a fork, then add the drained ricotta and the ... r the basil into pieces and add to the bowl. Season with salt, pepper and nutmeg ... ith a wooden spoon.

... olive oil in a frying pan – you should only have a film over the base – until it sizzles ... e of bread will turn golden brown immediately if the oil is hot enough). Tip the egg ... the pan and turn the heat down a little. Keep piercing the bottom of the mixture with ... e egg begins to set to allow the liquid on top to seep down. Cook until almost set.

... ve the pan from the heat, then, holding a dinner plate over the pan, flip the frittata onto ... Slide the frittata back into the pan with the undercooked side to the heat and cook for ... oment. Repeat the trick with the dinner plate and turn the frittata out to serve. (When I ... iis in my oval copper dish, as shown opposite, I can't perform the turning-out trick. Instead, ... the frittata off under a preheated griller in the oven for 5 minutes.)

... ccompany slices of the frittata with a salad of thickly sliced tomato and torn basil leaves ... ed with green and peppery extra-virgin olive oil, salt and pepper (I like adding rags of duck ... pasta to this salad, too – see page 40). Serves 4

toast sticks
'ornn ing)
ape Juice
we need
tchup
jur out)

you want
needed)
Chicken
or the
eek

The Wood Oven

The wood-oven saga began in the mid-1980s when we bought our cottage and surrounding land at Tanunda. We found we had inherited, right by the back door, the remains of a black kitchen, the Barossa term given to a small room often set away from the house in which a fire would feed an oven with a chimney, where wursts and hams were hung to smoke. There was, in fact, no chimney remaining, but the smoke-stained walls were enough to suggest we were right in our assumptions.

But, with no chimney and only one wall intact, the building couldn't remain as it was – it either had to go or be rebuilt. Keen to hang onto our bit of local history, we decided to reconstruct the kitchen using the existing rubble – but we chose a different site, and by moving it we opened up the view to the dam from the house. With our 'new' black kitchen in place, it soon became obvious that this was the perfect building in which to house a wood oven.

As there was no definitive oven to copy, we mistakenly tried to marry different styles of Barossa bread ovens, ending up with an igloo-shaped structure that emerged from the rear wall of the old kitchen. The oven burned very well but we could never stop it smoking. It smoked so badly that the cooking process was actually painful and the food always had a heavily smoked flavour. While smoked food is a great tradition in the Valley, this was beyond a joke. Everyone had a suggestion, and we tried several modifications. Finally we resorted to a change of culture and sought an Italian tradesman to build a wood-fired oven similar to those used by Italians the world over, whether they be keen home cooks or restaurateurs.

So, we now have a very traditional German cottage with a very traditional Italian wood oven, in which we can bake sixty loaves of bread at once, our builder assures us. I tried to write down all the advice he passed on to us over the three weekends it took to

build the oven, but as we didn't share a common language, the details are a bit sketchy.

We're still getting it right. In fact, the last time we fired up the oven for a late lunch in the courtyard, we had the fire raging far too early and by noon it was so fierce that we'd used enough wood for a whole day's cooking and the heat had cracked the metal door. At least we finally got to see one of the builder's main tips in operation: the brick in the middle of the third row, he said, must show white before the oven is hot enough to cook bread!

We light the fire hours before it is required and then scrape out the coals when we are ready to cook. At first we used to bucket the coals into a metal bin, all the time hating the waste. We've now built out of old bricks two shelves that run down either side of the oven. One side has a metre or so of shelf and a recess into which the hot coals can be transferred. A grill with handles hangs on the wall – this can be set at different heights above the coals so that we can grill the vegetables to accompany the offering in the oven. In fact, we grill anything from vegetables to chops, duck or mussels (page 208), as you can see Sophie doing opposite.

The second shelf is only about 30 cm wide, yet long enough to carry all the accompaniments and condiments we need. Our grandchildren like to choose their own toppings for the pizzas that emerge from the oven, so, aided by wooden boxes to stand on, this shelf is perfect for them.

One corner of the courtyard is now given over entirely to a supply of old vines, the result of grafting in the vineyard. These are wonderful fuel for the fire, and provide a bit of visual drama as rampant nasturtiums weave themselves through the gnarled trunks in a riot of colour, a contrast to the orderly cumquats in terracotta pots nearby.

It takes time to master the art of a wood oven, but it's the most communal way of cooking I know. I love the way many of our guests have looked around their own gardens to see if they can find a spot for one, too. Best of all was when Ann and Aldo Parronchi, friends from Chianti, home of the most amazing tradition of grills, fires and ovens, went home to add one to their own courtyard.

Yabby Tail Ravioli

Yabbies feature a lot at our place, whether we are just family or we're entertaining. But not everyone can cope with my enthusiasm: people, family included, are often horrified at the way I suck the mustard out of the heads of discarded yabbies when we're having one of our feasts! Serving yabby tail ravioli, then, is perfect for guests who aren't used to such performances.

12 cooked yabbies (page 47)

unsalted butter

⅓ cup sliced mushrooms

splash of verjuice

squeeze of lemon juice

2 tablespoons fresh white
  breadcrumbs

1 free-range egg white

duck egg pasta

270 g unbleached strong flour

6 free-range duck egg yolks

warm seafood dressing

1 shallot

125 ml verjuice

juice of 1 lemon

sea salt

freshly ground black pepper

120 ml extra-virgin olive oil

1 tablespoon freshly plucked
  chervil

To make the duck egg pasta, tip the flour onto a bench and make a well in the centre. Whisk the egg yolks and pour them into the well. Using a fork, incorporate the egg into the flour until the dough starts to come together, then use your hands. Knead the dough until it is shiny and firm to the touch, about 10 minutes. Form it into a ball, then flatten this into a disc. Wrap in plastic film and refrigerate for 30 minutes.

Meanwhile, prepare the base for the dressing. Slice the shallot finely. Reduce the verjuice, lemon juice and shallot over heat until ⅓ cup liquid remains. Remove the pan from the heat, then season with salt and pepper and set aside.

Cut the chilled pasta dough in half, then wrap one piece carefully in plastic film and freeze for another use. Using a pasta machine, roll the remaining dough through the settings until you reach the finest – cut the dough into 2 sheets once it starts to get too long to handle easily. Trim the ends of the pasta sheets to square them up, ensuring the sheets are the same length. Set aside under a clean tea towel until you are ready to proceed.

Peel the yabbies and roughly chop the tails. Heat a knob of butter in a frying pan and cook the mushrooms until softened, then deglaze the pan with the verjuice and lemon juice. Combine the yabby tails, mushrooms, pan juices and enough breadcrumbs to bind the mixture.

Bring a large saucepan of salted water to a boil. Meanwhile, remove any excess flour from the pasta and brush the sheets with lightly whisked egg white. Mark one sheet into 4 large squares, then divide the filling between these, mounding it in the middle of each one. Flatten out the filling a little. Position the other pasta sheet on top, gently pushing down between the mounds of filling to seal the parcels and to get rid of any air bubbles. Cut between each mound of filling to create 4 large ravioli.

Plunge the ravioli into the boiling water and bring the pan back to a boil – you may need to cook 2 ravioli only at a time. Simmer for 3 minutes, then drain well. While the ravioli are cooking, heat the dressing base in a non-reactive saucepan. Put a ravioli onto an entrée plate per person (or put 2 ravioli on a large plate if preparing a special lunch for 2 people), then swirl the olive oil and chervil into the base to complete the dressing and pour over the ravioli. Serve immediately. Serves 2–4

duck egg pasta   This became a speciality of mine simply because I always had lots of duck eggs. They make the richest, silkiest pasta imaginable, but you must use really good flour too. I've given a greater quantity than you need here, as leftovers can be frozen for another use. I love tossing 'rags' of this pasta through a tomato salad such as in the Ricotta and Basil Frittata recipe on page 35.

warm seafood dressing   This dressing can also be used with poached or grilled shellfish, such as marron, or even my mushroom or capsicum pâtés, using basil or flat-leaf parsley instead of chervil.

Pasta with Tuna and Zucchini Flowers

This is a gorgeous pasta dish for summer – the seared tuna is still pink and juicy, the lemon and capers add a really fresh zing, and the zucchini flowers provide colour and texture. Don't dismiss pumpkin flowers if you have them in the garden – they're larger and perhaps not as delicate as zucchini flowers but fine to use here.

8 shallots

extra-virgin olive oil

1 lemon

freshly ground black pepper

2 × 2.5 cm thick pieces
 trimmed tuna

4 zucchini flowers

1 tablespoon capers

280 g top-quality penne

sea salt

1–2 teaspoons unsalted butter

2 tablespoons freshly chopped
 flat-leaf parsley

Bring a small saucepan of water to a boil and blanch the shallots for 5 minutes. Allow to cool and then peel. Put the shallots into the tiniest saucepan or frying pan you have, then cover with olive oil and cook slowly until caramelised (you can also do this in the oven). Set aside.

Finely grate the lemon zest to yield 1 teaspoon, then juice the lemon. Mix the zest with some pepper and a little olive oil and pour this over the tuna, smearing it to coat, and leave for 20 minutes. Meanwhile, check the zucchini flowers are free of insects and wash very delicately. Allow to dry on kitchen paper. Wash the capers under running water to rid them of excess salt, then drain.

Cook the penne in a large saucepan of salted boiling water until al dente according to the manufacturer's instructions. Just before the pasta is cooked, drizzle a frying pan with a little olive oil and, when almost smoking-hot, sear the tuna for about 1 minute a side. Set aside on a plate while you attend to the pasta. Drain the pasta, then moisten it with olive oil to prevent it sticking.

Cut the resting tuna into 2.5 cm chunks. Melt the butter in the tuna pan, then quickly toss the zucchini flowers in this. Drain the caramelised shallots and toss with the tuna, zucchini flowers, capers, lemon juice, penne and parsley. (If the pasta has cooled quickly, warm it in a microwave or steamer and toss it with more olive oil before mixing it with the other ingredients.) Check for seasoning and serve immediately on entrée plates or in bowls. Serves 4

Cold Tomato Pasta

We first served this dish, among others, the night we had a wonderful party to celebrate the tenth birthday of the Pheasant Farm Restaurant. I love the natural 'saucing' that occurs when you let tomato, salt, pepper, basil and olive oil sit for a while at room temperature. While back in 1989 we served this 'sauce' with cooled Duck Egg Pasta (page 40), it's just as good with hot pasta.

1 kg vine-ripened tomatoes

2 cloves garlic

½ cup torn basil leaves

1 teaspoon sea salt

1 teaspoon sugar

extra-virgin olive oil

freshly ground black pepper

400 g penne

Core the tomatoes, then cut them into large dice. Mince the garlic cloves and toss through the tomato with the basil, salt, sugar and 125 ml olive oil, then season with pepper. Allow to sit for 2 hours at room temperature for the flavours to meld.

Meanwhile, cook the pasta in boiling salted water until al dente according to the manufacturer's instructions. Drain the pasta, then drizzle with olive oil to prevent it sticking and allow to cool to room temperature.

Toss the tomato mixture with the penne and taste for seasoning, then serve. Serves 4

optional extras   This dish can be extended in a multitude of ways: consider adding finely diced red onion or perhaps anchovy fillets, pitted olives or crumbled fresh ricotta or goat's curd.

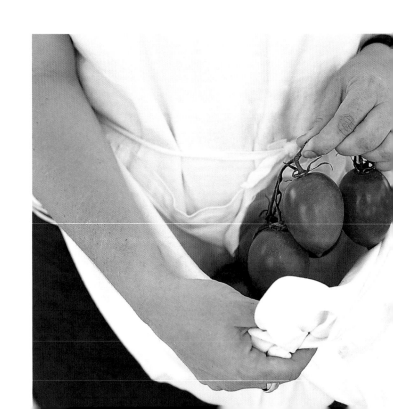

Basil Gnocchi with Warm Tomato Salsa

This dish began as a way of dealing with huge quantities of basil, not from my garden (I forget to break off the laterals) but from a friend's. While the tomato salsa makes for great summer eating, if you have any leftover gnocchi, pan-fry them in nut-brown butter, then add lashings of parmesan (these are good added to an antipasto plate, too).

unsalted butter

200 g unbleached plain flour

500 g waxy potatoes

sea salt

1 cup firmly packed basil
  leaves

freshly ground black pepper

warm tomato salsa

750 g ripe tomatoes

3 shallots

2 cloves garlic

3 sprigs thyme

100 g unsalted butter

extra-virgin olive oil

sea salt

freshly ground black pepper

¼ cup freshly chopped
  flat-leaf parsley

To make the salsa, core, seed and finely dice the tomatoes. Finely chop the shallots and garlic separately, then strip the leaves from the thyme. Cook the shallots in the butter and 1 tablespoon olive oil in a non-reactive saucepan until softened, then add the tomato, garlic and thyme and sauté briefly. Season with salt and pepper, then remove the pan from the heat. Set aside and keep warm.

Preheat the oven to 100°C and butter a serving dish. To make the gnocchi, spread the flour out into a rectangle on a bench. Peel the potatoes, then steam them until cooked right through. While still hot, pass them through a potato ricer or food mill so that the potato falls evenly over the flour. Sprinkle the potato with salt, then shred the basil finely and spread this over too. (Alternatively, blend the basil leaves and 1 tablespoon olive oil in a food processor, then drizzle this over the potato. This method produces a more even colour in the finished gnocchi.)

Melt 50 g butter and drizzle it evenly over the hot potato. Work the flour into the potato little by little using a pastry scraper until you have a firm dough. Knead the dough gently for 5 minutes. Divide the dough into quarters and roll each piece to make a long, thin sausage about 1 cm in diameter. Cut each sausage into 2.5 cm lengths.

Put the prepared serving dish into the oven to warm through. Gently warm the salsa.

I find a large, heavy-based 6 cm-deep baking dish perfect for poaching gnocchi. Fill such a dish with water, then bring it to a boil and add salt. When the water is boiling, raise the heat and quickly slip in all the gnocchi at once if the dish is large enough to take them in a single layer, then reduce the heat so that the water isn't too turbulent. Allow the gnocchi to cook for 1 minute after they have risen to the surface, then skim them out and put them into the warm serving dish and season. (If your poaching dish is not large enough to take the gnocchi in one layer, you will have to cook them in batches.)

Stir ¼ cup olive oil and the parsley through the salsa, then toss with the gnocchi, grind on pepper and serve immediately. Serves 4

an alternative   Try cooking 125 g butter until nut-brown, then toss the poached gnocchi in it until crisp. Forego the salsa and finish off the buttery juices with a little lemon juice or verjuice.

Marinated Octopus

Don't be scared to buy a whole giant octopus if you're feeding a crowd. Wrapped around a bowl of aïoli for your guests to carve and dip, the tentacles make a dramatic centrepiece for a buffet table. If this all seems too much, you can buy as little as one tentacle from your fishmonger, but only if you know it's been really well tumbled – or it will be as tough as old boots.

2 cloves garlic

¼ cup marjoram *or* oregano
   leaves

extra-virgin olive oil

2 large *or* 3 medium octopus
   tentacles

fresh marinade

180 ml extra-virgin olive oil

¼ cup red-wine vinegar

¼ cup freshly chopped
   flat-leaf parsley

sea salt

freshly ground black pepper

Chop the garlic and mix with the marjoram and a splash of olive oil in a shallow glass dish. Add the octopus and turn to coat thoroughly, then set aside for 1 hour. Meanwhile, preheat the barbecue.

Remove the octopus from the marinade and barbecue it for 25 minutes, turning it with a pair of long-handled tongs as often as required to ensure it caramelises evenly, until opaque but soft (it should feel similar to the heel of your palm).

Make the fresh marinade by combining all the ingredients in a clean glass dish, then marinate the cooked octopus in this for at least 20 minutes. Slice the octopus thinly and serve as part of an antipasto platter or make into a salad with rocket, cubed ripe tomato, marjoram and olives and dress with extra-virgin olive oil and lemon juice. Check for seasoning. **Serves 6**

Yabbies au Naturel

Serving freshly boiled yabbies on huge platters as we did at our summer party (see pages 10–15) is the essence of largesse to me. Most often, however, we end up eating yabbies au naturel on slabs of newspaper in a well-shaded spot, with two old wrought-iron wash-stands with enamelled basins as communal finger bowls. Eating yabbies like this is a messy business!

20 live yabbies

4 lemons

1 tablespoon dill seeds

fronds of dill *or* wild fennel

sea salt

extra-virgin olive oil

freshly ground black pepper

Stun the yabbies by putting them into the freezer in a tightly covered container for 20 minutes. Slice 2 of the lemons thickly and put into a large pot of water with the dill seeds and dill or fennel fronds and bring to a boil. Add 2 tablespoons salt.

When the water is boiling vigorously, slip in half the stunned yabbies and cover with a lid to bring the water back to a boil as quickly as possible. Remove the lid as soon as you reach boiling point or you'll have water cascading all over the stove. Scoop the yabbies out of the water and run them under cold water to inhibit the cooking process (I lower my yabbies into the pot in a wire basket with a handle, much like that used for pasta, which makes this job much easier). Let the water return to a boil before repeating the process with the remaining yabbies.

Serve the yabbies in a big bowl alongside a bottle of olive oil, the remaining lemons cut into wedges, sea salt and a pepper mill – and have plenty of really good crusty bread at hand for mopping up the extra oil and juices.

yabby heads   The next-best thing to devouring a freshly cooked yabby tail dunked in olive oil and squeezed with lemon juice is to pull the head apart to reveal the 'mustard'. Sucking on yabby heads truly divides real yabby lovers from the rest. I'm so addicted that I eat my own and then set about going through those discarded by the uninitiated!

Barbecued Sardines in Vine Leaves

Jim Mendolia, who produces wonderful tinned sardines and anchovies under the Auschovies label in Fremantle, answered my call for fresh sardines for these photographs. Ignoring catastrophes aboard his boat (a broken winch), he delivered the fish to Sophie Zalokar's verandah before dawn on the day she was flying to the Barossa to help me. Thanks, Jim!

fresh sardines

sea salt

freshly ground black pepper

medium-to-large fresh
  vine leaves

extra-virgin olive oil

lemon wedges

Gut but don't scale the sardines, and leave the heads and tails intact. Season the sardines with salt and pepper, then brush the vine leaves with olive oil. Wrap each sardine in a vine leaf and brush the outside of the leaf with olive oil.

Preheat a barbecue to high. Put some of the wrapped sardines into a hinged wire grill (the sort used when camping) and cook for 3–4 minutes on the first side, depending on the size of the sardines, then turn and cook the other side. (If the fire is fierce, you will only need to cook the sardines for 2 minutes a side.) Rest the sardines away from the heat for 5 minutes. As the parcel is unwrapped, the skin and scales will come away with the leaf. Serve with plenty of lemon wedges and a large fingerbowl of hot water – this is definitely outside eating.

skewers   If you don't have a hinged grill, soak long wooden skewers in water for 1 hour. Run a skewer through each end of the fish, then add as many wrapped sardines as will fit, leaving a little space between each. Grill as above.

fresh sardines   Sardines must be snapping fresh to be at their best. Look for super-shiny, taut fish with clear, clear eyes, and ask your fishmonger how long ago they left the boat. Sardines just out of the water can be scaled and barbecued whole, guts and all, as the flesh peels away from the bone. Sardines this fresh are also fabulous served raw (after they've been scaled and gutted and you've slipped their bones out with your fingers) with a drizzle of fruity extra-virgin olive oil, a squeeze of lemon juice and a sprinkle of sea salt and freshly ground black pepper.

marinade   Wonderful as they are without any adornment, sardines can also be marinated before barbecuing. Try tossing them with freshly chopped flat-leaf parsley, dill, oregano or even thyme, and some lemon zest, freshly ground black pepper and a little olive oil and leave them to sit for 30 minutes–1 hour before cooking. The dried oregano available in Greek or Middle Eastern food stores would be a fragrant option.

Cured Side of Salmon

If we are in Adelaide on a Friday night we often buy a side of salmon and cart it home in an Esky to share with the family. We slice the thick end super-fine to eat raw with sea salt, good olive oil and perhaps something acidic, and then we sugar-cure the tail. But for a party, there's nothing more inviting – or simple to prepare – than a whole side of cured salmon.

1 × 1.25 kg trimmed side of
  salmon (skin removed)
150 g sea salt
150 g white *or* soft light-brown
  sugar
1 cup roughly chopped dill *or*
  wild fennel (including
  flowerheads, if available)

Using tweezers, remove the line of large bones visible in the salmon. Choose 2 large non-reactive dishes or trays the length of the salmon (I use plastic butcher's trays), then mix the salt, sugar and dill or fennel and spread half over the base of one of the dishes. Put the salmon on top of this, then cover with the remaining dill mixture. Cover tightly with plastic film, then put the second dish on top of the fish and weight this. Transfer the salmon and weight to the refrigerator.

How long you decide to cure the fish for will depend on how moist you want to serve it. I cure mine for about 8 hours on average, but once I forgot it and left it for 20 hours! At this stage it was much drier but the positive was that it was less challenging for people unsure about the rawness of salmon cured for a shorter time.

Wipe the salt and sugar from the salmon with a wet clean cloth or one moistened with a little olive oil. Some of the dill or fennel will remain adhered to the salmon. Carve the fish and serve with slices of lemon, horseradish cream or vinaigrette, or the salsa that partners the poached salmon opposite. **Serves 8**

Salmon Poached in Olive Oil with Tomato and Avocado Salsa

This is a very special, even sensuous dish. It works best when the salmon fillets are the same size and weight (ideally from the middle of the fish). The cooked salmon is quite pink inside and warm rather than hot, so make sure your guests don't belong to the 'if it's not piping hot, it's not right' school of thought!

4 trimmed salmon fillets

extra-virgin olive oil

sea salt

tomato and avocado salsa

4 small ripe tomatoes

1 very small red onion

½ large Reed avocado

6 basil leaves

250 ml mellow extra-virgin
  olive oil

juice of 1 lemon

sea salt

freshly ground black pepper

To make the salsa, core and seed the tomatoes and cut them into small dice (to yield about 1 cup). Cut the onion and avocado into dice the same size, and tear the basil into pieces. Combine these ingredients with the olive oil and lemon juice, then season with salt and pepper and set aside at room temperature for the flavours to meld.

Remove the skin from the salmon fillets, if present, then extract any bones with tweezers. Choose a heavy-based saucepan or deep frying pan large enough to take the fish – the smaller the pan, the less olive oil you will need to use. Pour a generous amount of olive oil into the pan, then stand it over a very low heat and bring to blood temperature only (dip your finger into the oil – it should not feel hot). Slip the fillets into the oil – they should lie just below the surface like submarines – and cook at this gentle temperature for 18–22 minutes. If white dots appear on the surface of the fish, the oil is too hot (these are beads of protein).

Remove the salmon from the pan with an egg slice and put straight onto waiting plates. Mound some salsa on top of each fillet and serve immediately with sea salt on the table. The salmon will be quite pink in the centre but will be cooked. **Serves 4**

Barbecued Quail in a Fig Bath

Steeping grilled quail in a fresh marinade is a technique I've long loved – the beauty of it is that the flavourings can be altered according to what you have to hand. Instead of dried figs, you could add grapes and roasted walnuts, or perhaps raisins that have been reconstituted in red-wine vinegar and then tossed in nut-brown butter with some rosemary. A recipe is just an idea, after all.

8 quail

extra-virgin olive oil

freshly ground black pepper

2 lemons

fig bath

8 tiny white *or* 4 larger dried
 figs

verjuice

2 lemons

125 ml extra-virgin olive oil

1 cup basil leaves

freshly ground black pepper

Using kitchen shears, cut away the backbone from each quail and slip out the rib cage with your fingers. Rub each bird with a little olive oil, then season with pepper and allow to sit for 1 hour before grilling.

Meanwhile, preheat a barbecue or prepare your fire, allowing it to burn down to glowing embers. Start to prepare the fig bath by reconstituting the figs in enough verjuice to cover them for 20 minutes, then drain and cut them in half (or quarters, if using larger figs). Remove the zest from the lemons using a potato peeler, then juice 1 lemon. Set aside.

Grill the quail, turning them frequently, for about 8 minutes in all, depending on the heat of the fire. While the quail are cooking, finish preparing the fig bath by pouring the olive oil into a shallow glass dish, then adding the figs, lemon zest and juice. Chop the basil finely and add it to the bath with a good grinding of pepper. Transfer the cooked quail to the bath and rest, turning once or twice, for 10 minutes before serving with the freekah salad on page 32. **Serves 4**

dried white figs   Look for imported tiny dried white figs in Middle Eastern food stores.

Chicken Pieces with Preserved Lemon, Pancetta and Rosemary

A family favourite for a long time, this dish was to be the main event at our summer party for sixty (see pages 10–15) at which we wanted to show off our new wood-fired oven. But on the day we found ourselves ferrying the baking dishes inside to the double oven, as we hadn't quite come to grips with controlling the temperature of the other!

10 × 375 g free-range chicken
   Marylands
8 quarters preserved lemon
⅓ cup finely chopped rosemary
125 ml extra-virgin olive oil
freshly ground black pepper
12 thin slices pancetta

Cut the drumsticks away from the thighs. Remove the pulp from the preserved lemon, then rinse and cut into small dice. Toss the chicken pieces in 2 shallow baking dishes with the preserved lemon, rosemary and olive oil, then grind over pepper. Allow the chicken to sit for 1 hour for the flavours to infuse.

Meanwhile, preheat the oven to 230°C. Make sure the chicken pieces are lying skin-side up, then bake for 15 minutes. Turn the chicken over and swap the positions of the trays. Cook for another 10 minutes, then test for doneness. (The chicken will continue cooking while it rests, but if the juices run very pink when you prick the thickest part of the thigh, you may want to return the meat to the oven for a few more minutes.) Turn the chicken over to be skin-side up again and rest, covered with foil, for 15 minutes.

Meanwhile, crisp the pancetta on a baking tray in the oven for 10 minutes, then add to the resting chicken. Serve the chicken and pancetta with a salad and good crusty bread. **Serves 10**

sauce   If you wish to serve a sauce with this, add 125 ml hot reduced chicken stock and ¼ cup verjuice to the baking dishes while the chicken is resting.

chicken pieces   I've used Marylands here, but if you have the chance to buy the thighs alone, they're probably an even better option. Don't forget to buy chicken in any form with the skin on: if you're strong-willed enough you can remove it after cooking, but the skin and fat keep the meat beautifully moist and impart flavour during cooking.

Chook Roasted with Garlic and Verjuice

I never use anything other than a well-brought-up chook. The flavour and texture are so incredibly different from that of a mass-produced bird that you'd wonder whether they were the same species. But note that there is little point buying a free-range chook under 2 kg: the smaller birds haven't had the time to develop these exceptional qualities (the one pictured below came in at 4 kg!).

30 cloves garlic

water

1 lemon

1 × 2.5 kg free-range chicken

3 sprigs rosemary

sea salt

freshly ground black pepper

verjuice

50 ml extra-virgin olive oil

Preheat the oven to 230°C. Blanch the unpeeled garlic in boiling water for 5 minutes, then drain.

Cut the lemon in half and squeeze the juice into the cavity of the chicken, then add the rosemary and season with salt and pepper. Mix 50 ml verjuice with the olive oil and some salt and pepper, then brush this over the skin of the bird. Sit the chook on a trivet in a shallow baking dish (about 5 cm deep), then transfer to the middle shelf of the oven and cook for 20 minutes.

Reduce the oven temperature to 180°C and pour 125 ml verjuice and 125 ml water over the chicken and put the blanched garlic into the bottom of the baking dish. Cook for another 20 minutes, then reduce the oven temperature to 120°C and add another 125 ml verjuice and 125 ml water (doing this stops the juices burning in the baking dish). Cook for another 20 minutes, then turn the chook over to brown the underside for 10 minutes. Remove the chook to a warm serving plate and cover well with foil, then allow to rest for 25 minutes.

Pour all the juices in the baking dish into a tall, narrow jug, then refrigerate this while the chicken is resting. Just before serving, scoop away the fat that has risen to the top, then warm the remaining jus. Carve the chook, then pour over the jus and serve with the roasted garlic, boiled waxy potatoes and a bitter green salad. Serves 6

Turkey with Apple and Prune Stuffing and Glazed Chestnuts

Can I admit that I had never cooked a turkey before I came up with this recipe? Turkey isn't part of our Christmas fare, and if offered it elsewhere I'd ask for the stuffing and pass on the bird, only knowing dry meat with little flavour. What a difference a corn-fed free-range turkey makes! The big surprise was the oven bag – it produced such a moist and luscious bird that it converted me immediately.

1 × 5.6 kg free-range, corn-fed
  turkey
65 g finely sliced prosciutto
½ teaspoon unbleached
  plain flour
2 kg frozen peeled chestnuts
2.2 litres chicken stock
500 ml wine
50 g butter

apple and prune stuffing
100 g dried apple
100 ml verjuice
2 large brown onions
200 g pitted prunes
180 g chicken livers
15 g butter
125 ml extra-virgin olive oil
1 small handful flat-leaf parsley
2 sprigs rosemary
2–3 sprigs thyme
12 sage leaves
4½ cups fresh white
  breadcrumbs
sea salt
freshly ground black pepper

Preheat the oven to 180°C. To make the stuffing, roughly chop the dried apple and reconstitute it in the verjuice until soft, then drain. Finely chop the onions (to yield about 410 g) and chop the prunes. Clean the chicken livers, then melt the butter in a frying pan and seal the livers until golden brown but still very pink in the middle. Remove the pan from the heat and rest the livers for 5 minutes, then cut them into large chunks. Add the olive oil to the pan and cook the onion until translucent.

Finely chop the parsley (you need 2 tablespoons), rosemary (1 tablespoon), thyme (1 tablespoon) and sage (2 tablespoons). In a large bowl, combine the freshly chopped herbs, breadcrumbs, onion, liver, prunes and apple, then season with salt and pepper. Fill the cavity of the turkey, and lay the prosciutto over the breast. Truss the turkey well with kitchen string.

Put the flour into an oven bag, then give the bag a shake and tip out any excess flour. Slide the turkey into the oven bag, repairing the prosciutto if any slices shift in the process. Tie the end of the bag well with kitchen string and slip it into another oven bag, then seal this too. Bake the turkey in its oven bags in a baking dish for 2½ hours. Remove the turkey from the oven and allow to rest breast down for 1 hour in its oven bags; the turkey will retain its heat during the resting time, so reheating is unnecessary.

Meanwhile, simmer the chestnuts in the chicken stock until tender, about 20 minutes. Drain and reserve 2 litres of the cooking liquor. Bring the reserved cooking liquor, wine and butter to a boil in a non-reactive saucepan and reduce until thick and syrupy. Add the chestnuts to the glaze and warm through.

Serve the turkey on a large platter with the glazed chestnuts to the side. Don't forget the stuffing! Serves 12–16

frozen chestnuts   I make this using Cheznutz, frozen peeled chestnuts available by mail order from an enterprising couple in Victoria's north-east (check out the Cheznutz website). Having these in the freezer is so convenient that I've become lazy and now tend only to buy fresh chestnuts for roasting over an open fire in my much-favoured iron pan that has holes in the base for just this purpose.

Barbecued Lamb's Kidneys in Caul with Bay Leaves

The courtyard off our kitchen is where we do a lot of our eating – it's where our wood oven and grill are, so we never need much of an excuse to get out there. As the bay tree is in the courtyard, too, I prepare these little parcels outside and serve them as a prelude to the main event while we stand around with a drink in hand.

100 g caul fat

8 lamb's kidneys

8 fresh bay leaves

freshly ground black pepper

50 ml extra-virgin olive oil

sea salt

Preheat the barbecue; if using a wood fire, make sure the fire has burned down to a bed of glowing embers.

Lay the caul fat out on a chopping board and cut it into sizes suitable to wrap up each kidney. Put a bay leaf right-side down in the centre of each piece of caul fat, then put a whole kidney on top of the bay leaf and grind over some pepper. Wrap the caul fat around each kidney to make 8 little parcels. Brush with the olive oil and barbecue for 5–7 minutes, depending on the heat of the fire, turning the parcels halfway through cooking. (You can also thread the parcels onto wooden skewers that have been soaked in water for an hour beforehand and then barbecue them on these.)

Serve hot with a pot of sea salt alongside – great snack food around the barbecue. Cold left-overs are a treat, too! Serves 4

caul fat   Caul fat is the fine fatty membrane that lines the abdominal cavity of animals (pork caul is the best). It is wonderful for wrapping all sorts of meats as it crisps beautifully during cooking and melts away to nothing – my friend Cath Kerry calls it 'nature's Gladwrap'. I always have some in my freezer – you can order it from your butcher, but need to soak it overnight in salted water to rid it of all blood before using or freezing.

Marinated Boned Lamb for the Barbecue

I'm lucky enough to have access to milk-fed lamb through Barossa Farm Produce, my elder daughter Saskia's business. The caramelisation that barbecuing creates provides a wonderful contrast to this naturally sweet and tender lamb. Boning the leg to create an even 'rectangle' of meat makes cooking and carving even easier, and resting the grilled meat in a marinade adds yet another flavour dimension.

1 × 1.5 kg boned leg of
  milk-fed lamb

marinade

1 large quarter preserved
  lemon

2 shallots

2 sprigs rosemary

250 ml verjuice

⅓ cup extra-virgin olive oil

juice of 1 lemon

sea salt

freshly ground black pepper

To make the marinade, remove the pulp from the preserved lemon, then rinse and chop the rind. Chop the shallots, then mix with the remaining marinade ingredients.

If the butcher hasn't boned the leg of lamb, do so now to produce a rectangle of meat. Rearrange the meat where necessary to produce a similar thickness all over. Pour half the marinade into a flat glass dish, then add the lamb and pour in the remaining marinade. Leave to marinate for several hours.

Preheat the oven to 200°C and preheat the barbecue; if using a wood fire, ensure the flames have burned down to a bed of glowing embers.

Remove the meat from the marinade and wipe off any excess. Treating the meat as a whole slab, put it skin-side down onto the barbecue and cook until it is well seared and coloured. Turn it over and sear the other side. Repeat this, making sure no part is becoming too charcoaled. It takes me 25 minutes to barbecue a milk-fed lamb leg – the size of the leg will dictate the cooking time. Transfer the leg to a baking dish and cook it in the oven for 10 minutes, then allow it to rest for 10 minutes before carving. Serves 4–6

resting marinade   For an extra burst of flavour, make up half a batch of fresh marinade and rest the cooked lamb in this for 10 minutes before serving. The juices from the meat mingle with the marinade to produce a delicious 'sauce'.

Slow-cooked Lamb Shanks with Verjuice, Preserved Lemon, Bay Leaves, Rosemary and Garlic

One advantage of having a farmer/broker in the family is that I get to cook the bits people seldom order, and these cuts are often those we love more than any others. The shanks from Saskia's Barossa Farm Produce milk-fed lambs are so amazingly sweet and tender that I cook them in verjuice. If using larger shanks, try 3 parts chicken stock to I part verjuice instead.

17 cloves garlic

8 milk-fed lamb shanks

12 sprigs rosemary

extra-virgin olive oil

5 quarters preserved lemon

8 bay leaves

500 ml verjuice

1 teaspoon peppercorns

1 teaspoon sea salt

Preheat the oven to 120°C. Finely chop 3 of the garlic cloves and put them into a heavy-based non-reactive pot with the shanks, rosemary and a splash of olive oil. Brown the meat on the stove over a low heat, turning it regularly.

Remove the pulp from the preserved lemons, then rinse the rind and cut each piece in half. Put the preserved lemon and remaining ingredients into the pot with the shanks and stir to mix. Cover the pot with a lid, then bake very slowly for 4 hours.

The shanks and their juices are delicious served with the freekah salad on page 32, as shown here. **Serves 4**

Barbecued Kangaroo Fillet with Onions and Wine Butter

I love the distinctive iron-y, gamy flavour of kangaroo. This dense meat has virtually no fat, so it must be cooked very quickly or it will be as tough as old boots. Kangaroo fillets are particularly suited to the barbecue, as long as they've been coated with oil before cooking and are well rested afterwards.

16 pickling onions

verjuice

20 fresh bay leaves

4 × 250 g trimmed kangaroo
  fillets

extra-virgin olive oil

freshly ground black pepper

wine butter

250 ml red wine

125 ml port

125 g softened unsalted butter

¼ cup finely chopped chives

To make the wine butter, reduce the wine and port over heat until almost a glaze, then allow to cool. Mix the cooled glaze into the butter, then add the chives (fingers are best, but be warned – you'll look like a winemaker during vintage!). Form the butter into a log, then wrap it in foil and freeze for 30 minutes until hard.

Soak 4 wooden skewers in water for 30 minutes. Blanch the onions in a non-reactive saucepan in enough verjuice to cover them until just soft, then allow to cool before peeling them. Starting with a bay leaf, thread the bay leaves and onions alternately onto the skewers, allowing 4 onions and 5 bay leaves per skewer. Set aside.

Meanwhile, trim the kangaroo fillets if you have not bought them trimmed. Smear the fillets quickly with olive oil and grind on pepper, then cover with plastic film and allow to sit for 20 minutes before cooking. (You need to coat the kangaroo thoroughly as the meat oxidises very quickly once cut or removed from its vacuum packaging.)

Preheat the barbecue to high, or stand a frying pan over a high heat. Cook the fillets for 3 minutes on the first side (don't turn before this or the flesh will stick and tear), then turn and cook for another 2–3 minutes, depending on the thickness of the meat. Allow to rest in a warm spot for a good 6–8 minutes with a slice of wine butter melting on top.

Meanwhile, brush the onion and bay skewers with olive oil, then grill, turning regularly, until caramelised. Serve a kangaroo fillet per person with a fresh slice of wine butter on top (or alternatively take a pot of the butter to the table) and a skewer alongside. **Serves 4**

Rillettes

People frightened of fat are unlikely to try these, but they are the losers! Cooking and preserving meat in fat (whether it's rabbit, hare, goose, duck or even chook) is a staple of my kitchen as it's the best way of using the legs, the least-tender meat of all. Mustard fruits, pickled quince (page 182) or onion confit make a good partner to rillettes.

3 rabbits

55 g sea salt

2 tablespoons fresh thyme
  leaves

1 tablespoon juniper berries

2 teaspoons peppercorns

500 ml rendered chicken *or*
  duck fat

Joint the rabbits, leaving the saddles, kidneys and livers for another dish. Combine the legs, shoulders and seasonings in a glass dish and leave for several hours.

Preheat the oven to 160°C. Put the legs into the bottom of the heaviest-based pot you have, then add the shoulders. Melt the rendered fat in a saucepan, then pour enough of this over the rabbit to just cover the meat. Cover tightly and cook in the oven for 4–5 hours, stirring occasionally. The rabbit must cook very slowly and must never boil, otherwise it will toughen.

Drain the fat from the cooking pot and strain it into a container. The meat should be falling off the bone. Shred the meat with 2 forks, discarding the bones. When the fat is nearly cold, pour enough over the meat to bind it together. Check for seasoning – rillettes are traditionally highly seasoned. Pack the rillettes into glass or china dishes. If sealed with a layer of melted fat, they will keep refrigerated for up to 3 weeks. Serve the rillettes with cornichons and toast or Fig and Prune Mustard (page 104). **Makes 750 ml**

rendered fat   To render the chicken or duck fat needed for this recipe, trim 5 kg of carcasses of all fat and skin. (The amount of fat on a carcass varies from breed to breed and according to feeding programs. If you haven't enough carcasses to render your own fat, buy fatty duck necks from a duck processor instead. Luv-a-duck, in fact, now sells its own rendered duck fat by the kilo, if you don't have the time or inclination.) Put the fat and skin into a saucepan and add enough water to just cover. Bring the pan to a boil, then reduce to a simmer and cook for about 45 minutes until the water has evaporated and golden, crispy solids are visible in the clear, liquid fat. Allow to cool a little, then strain and discard the solids from the fat. Cover and refrigerate the rendered fat – it lasts for months! Rendered fat is delicious when used to crisp sautéing potatoes.

Flatbread

Flatbread makes great party food – pull the hot flatbread from the oven, then coat each one with really good extra-virgin olive oil and let your guests add a little sea salt and pepper or slices of really ripe tomato. This involves everyone in the kitchen and gets them licking their fingers!

15 g fresh *or* 1½ teaspoons
  dried yeast
½ teaspoon sugar (optional)
375 ml warm water
500 g unbleached strong flour
2 tablespoons wholemilk
  powder
1½ teaspoons sea salt
extra-virgin olive oil
¼ cup polenta (optional)

If using fresh yeast, combine it with the sugar and 1 tablespoon of the warm water in a small bowl, then dissolve the yeast by mashing it with a fork and set aside for 5–10 minutes until frothy.

Mix the flour, milk powder and salt in a large bowl, then make a well in the centre and add ¼ cup olive oil and the yeast mixture (if you are using dried yeast, add it now with the oil but omit the sugar). Pour in the remaining warm water and stir until well combined, then turn the dough out onto a floured bench and knead for about 10 minutes until shiny and smooth. Return the dough to the lightly oiled bowl, then cover the bowl with plastic film and allow the dough to double in size again in a draught-free spot – this will take about 1½ hours.

Turn the dough out, then knock it back and knead again for a few minutes and divide into 6 pieces. Roll each piece into a ball and allow these to rest under a tea towel for 15 minutes. Grease baking trays with oil or sprinkle them with polenta. Spread each ball of dough into a round about 1 cm thick. Brush the rounds with olive oil, then 'dimple' the tops with your fingertips. Cover the dough with tea towels and allow to double in size again, 45 minutes–1 hour.

Meanwhile, preheat the oven to 220°C with an unglazed terracotta or pizza tile in it, if you have one. Bake the flatbread for 15 minutes if using a tile, or 18 minutes if using baking trays. Top the hot flatbread with your favourite ingredients (see below) – or let your visitors do it themselves – and eat immediately. **Makes 6**

toppings   Have a variety of toppings ready for when the flatbread is cooked: really good extra-virgin olive oil, freshly sliced ripe tomato, bunches of fresh herbs, Parmigiano-Reggiano, anchovies, and so on. One of our favourites is lots and lots of freshly chopped herbs or rocket piled high on the warm bread and dressed with vinaigrette.

pizzas   This dough can also be used to make 8 very thin or 4 thick pizza bases. After the dough has doubled in size, knead it for 1–2 minutes, then divide it into 4–8 pieces and roll out each one until 17 cm in diameter. Let your guests add their own toppings, then cook the pizzas for 10–12 minutes at 230°C. We make pizzas with our little grandchildren every Sunday evening we happen to be home – they love adding their favourite toppings, and I love seeing them so involved.

The Bakery

It was the right morning to visit the Apex Bakery in Tanunda – the first cool day after a heatwave that broke all records. As I parked the car, the smell of freshly baked bread filled the air: no wonder, as several trolleys, each with a dozen trays holding four large loaves, had been pushed outside for the bread to cool.

Albert Hoffmann established the Apex in 1924, and 12-year-old Keith Fechner (known as Chiney) started work there soon after. These days Chiney's three sons are in charge: Brian (or Nipper) and twins Jonathan and David.

To walk into this bakery is to step back in time. Albert's huge, domed Scottish wood-fired oven is still in place – Mallee wood fuels the fire and a firebox, with the help of flues, creates the draft that pulls the flames across the roof. The floor of the oven is made up of fire bricks and sand – no mortar here. The firebricks in the dome have only been replaced once in the oven's lifetime, and that was back in 1971. The oven itself is so huge it can take 500 traditional high-loaf tins.

The oven temperature is measured in Fahrenheit and the original recipes are still in use, so much so that the young apprentices learn to weigh out pounds and ounces with the old cast-iron weights. Even the original black tins and trays are used every day. Piles and piles of tins rest upside-down on each other; those not used frequently are covered with a protective layer of flour dust – respect for equipment is never greater than in a family-owned business. The shovel that has stood by the fire door since 1924 is half eaten away from carrying burning embers outside when the fire needs to be dulled quickly; the hand-forged crowbar used for poking the coals apart when the fire needs to be reinvigorated stands alongside.

Bread, made with fabulous flour from Laucke, the local mill, is the mainstay of the Apex. The boys

are proud of their natural, slow ferment, which Jonathan gets going every night between 11 p.m. and midnight, with the rest of the team arriving at 3 a.m. Ensuring the oven is ready at the same time as the dough finishes proving is an art, the heat of the fire depending on the density of the wood. The bread is baked at 500°F (260°C), although for about 25 years the pyrometer was broken and the boys simply stuck their hands into the oven to gauge the temperature! During this time I saw them use newspaper 'hats' to stop the loaves from scorching.

The Apex has made a Barossa favourite called streuselkuchen since it first opened. This yeast cake is made in great slabs, with or without fruit. Apricots top it in early summer, followed as the season progresses by red grapes and then plums. The Fechners have a huge plum tree in their garden and they freeze the fruit whole. Halved and stoned, it thaws on the streusel before it all goes into the oven, the juices bleeding into the cake. Hot from the oven, this is addictive, let me tell you! On my last visit, Nipper deftly halved and then filled a huge slab of bienenstich with cream, a tradition begun by Martin Meinel in the 1960s. Martin used to bake bienenstich this way at home for the local men's choir; when he retired he made it at the Apex. A yeast cake, it has a honey and almond crust and is filled with cream or custard. The old-timer wouldn't pass on the recipe, but David used to watch carefully from the next room and guessed the ingredients and measures. Martin died in the mid-1980s, and today bienenstich is found in every Valley bakery.

Nipper and his family are always ready to try anything. I approached him years ago about making bread during vintage using shiraz lees as the yeast – a difficult thing to do now that stainless steel fermentation tanks have taken over from open fermenters. Not only was he happy to do it, but he knew the exact process required as his father had made streuselkuchen this way for locals many years ago! Since then my special feasts have featured this marvellous bread, and during vintage it is available from the bakery on request.

This spirit of generosity extends beyond the walls of the bakery, and the Fechner boys can always be counted on to be part of community events. One memorable year, Thea Schubert, who pulled off miracles when organising so much of the early music festivals, was keen to wow interstate journalists visiting for the winter launch of the festival program by taking them up to Menglers Hill to see the Barossa spread before them. It was the winter solstice – the sun was shining but it was chillingly cold, and the fortified wine brought along from Orlando by Bruce Thiele, another great festival supporter, was much appreciated. Then, chugging up the hill came the Apex's beautifully restored, bright-yellow 1926 Chevrolet delivery van! Out stepped Johnnie, who opened the back door and passed around warm streuselkuchen. Without the support of people like the Fechners, the Barossa Music Festival and other Valley highlights would never be as rich.

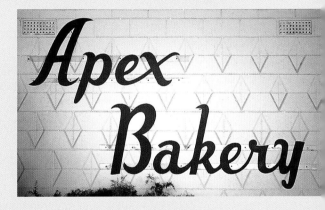

Orange Pound Cake with Passionfruit Icing

A pound cake is satisfyingly heavy and yet so moist, and the citrus used here makes it fresh, too. Passionfruit icing is my favourite of all, whether it's on this pound cake or on a light-as-a-feather sponge. I can't resist the piquant sweetness of passionfruit, and it just *smells* of summer!

230 g softened cream cheese

230 g softened unsalted butter

330 g castor sugar

finely grated zest of 2 oranges

4 × 61 g free-range eggs

350 g unbleached plain flour

2 teaspoons baking powder

¼ teaspoon salt

2 tablespoons sour cream

2 teaspoons pure vanilla
   extract

passionfruit icing

50 g unsalted butter

pulp of 2 passionfruit

180 g icing sugar

Preheat the oven to 180°C and grease and line 2 large loaf tins. Beat the cream cheese and butter with the castor sugar and orange zest in an electric mixer until pale, thick and creamy. Slowly add the eggs, one at a time, beating well after each addition.

Sift the flour with the baking powder and salt and gently beat into the mixture. Add the sour cream and vanilla extract and continue to beat until well incorporated. Spoon the batter into the prepared tins and bake for 35–45 minutes until a skewer comes away clean when inserted into the middle of the cake. Turn out onto a wire rack to cool completely before icing.

To make the passionfruit icing, melt the butter, then stir in the passionfruit pulp and add the mixture to the icing sugar. Put into a microwave oven and, giving it short bursts, heat just enough to make the icing molten but not too thin. If you don't have a microwave oven, just make the icing in the butter saucepan and warm it very gently on the stove. Pour the icing over the cooled cakes and allow to set before cutting. **Serves 12–15**

turkey eggs   This cake is sublime when made with turkey eggs (see opposite). It would also be great if made with duck eggs. If you have either, you'll need 3 duck eggs or 2½ turkey eggs (whisk 3 and measure off one-sixth, using the balance). Both turkey and duck eggs are rich and voluminous when beaten into cake batters.

Passionfruit Soufflé

Guests are always impressed when I offer a soufflé, and to make sure everyone enjoys the drama of it all I only serve them when we're eating in the kitchen. I'd hate to lose that theatrical flourish when I remove the soufflé in full puff from the oven or the incredible smells that burst forth and linger in the air as everyone tucks in.

unsalted butter

castor sugar

300 ml milk

2 tablespoons unbleached
  plain flour

1 pinch salt

5 free-range egg yolks

100 ml passionfruit pulp

6 free-range egg whites

Preheat the oven to 180°C. Melt 1 teaspoon butter in a saucepan, then brush a large soufflé dish with this and sprinkle in a little castor sugar. Roll the dish around to coat the insides evenly with the castor sugar and shake out any excess. (If your soufflé dish is not large, make a collar from a doubled layer of baking paper and wrap it around the outside of the bowl so that it stands above the rim, then secure with kitchen string.)

Heat the milk in a small saucepan. Bring another small saucepan of water to a boil and stand a stainless steel bowl over it. Melt 40 g butter in the bowl, then whisk in the flour and salt. Gradually add the hot milk while whisking vigorously. Cook the batter over the simmering water for 8 minutes, stirring occasionally and ensuring the water continues to simmer gently. Remove the bowl from the heat and allow to cool a little.

Whisk the egg yolks, passionfruit pulp and ¼ cup castor sugar into the slightly cooled batter. In another bowl or an electric mixer, whisk the egg whites until soft peaks form. Take a large spoonful of the egg whites and fold them into the batter, then tip the batter into the bowl with the remaining egg whites and fold it in with a whisk. Gently spoon the batter into the prepared dish using a metal spoon and cook for 40 minutes. It is imperative that you do not open the oven door while the soufflé is cooking! This is a major reason why soufflés do not rise to their full glory.

Remove the soufflé from the oven and serve immediately with extra passionfruit pulp and pouring cream alongside. Serves 4

preparing in advance   You can make the base of the soufflé a couple of hours beforehand and leave it at room temperature until required, then whisk the egg whites and proceed as above.

Verjuice Sorbet

Serving sorbet as a cleanser between courses isn't particularly fashionable these days, but on a hot summer's day, a verjuice sorbet made from the early grapes of the season is incredibly refreshing. In the summer of 2001, when the mercury hovered over 40°C for days on end, Col would eat this for afternoon tea.

1 litre verjuice

2 tablespoons glucose

Bring the verjuice and glucose to a boil in a non-reactive saucepan and simmer for 2 minutes. Allow to cool, then refrigerate until chilled.

Churn the chilled mixture in an ice-cream machine according to the manufacturer's instructions. Serve immediately or within 2 days. If stored for longer than this, the sorbet loses its acidity and delicate flavour. The longer it is frozen, the harder it will be, too. Serves 6–8

Berries in Jelly

I first revelled in a dish similar to this in Cath Kerry's café at the Art Gallery of South Australia. Cath had used shiraz and spices. Wanting to make a particularly Barossa statement, I have since extended the idea and use sparkling shiraz, which has strong, spicy overtones. I would have liked to use Rockford's Black Shiraz but thought better of it – I'd prefer to savour it in the glass!

750 ml sparkling shiraz

300 g sugar

8 gelatine leaves

2 punnets of berries

Bring the wine to a boil in a non-reactive saucepan, then light a match and touch it to the surface to burn off the alcohol. Turn off the heat and stir in the sugar until dissolved. Set the pan aside for 30 minutes to cool.

Soften the gelatine leaves in a small bowl of cold water for 5 minutes. Add the softened leaves to the cooled wine mixture and stir over a low heat just enough to dissolve the gelatine, then remove from the heat and allow to cool.

Pour a little of the cooled jelly mixture into the base of your chosen bowl or mould (it should hold about 2 litres) and allow it to just set in the refrigerator. Arrange a layer of berries on top, then add a little more jelly to cover the fruit. Refrigerate until set. Continue to build up the layers of berries by allowing them to set in the jelly before adding more. This will ensure the berries are evenly dispersed through the jelly. (If the remaining jelly starts to become too firm before you need it, simply warm it a little and then allow it to cool before adding the next layer of jelly and berries.)

Spoon the jellied berries from the bowl, or turn out the jelly by dipping the base of the mould into hot water and then inverting it over a waiting plate. Serve with double cream. Serves 8–10

berries   The ripeness of the berries used is much more important than the variety, so choose the very best you can.

Cherry Clafoutis

Cherries seem to get better and better each year. The dark, very juicy varieties are my favourites and are a perfect foil to a clafoutis batter. This is not a heavy dessert, but I tend to serve it early in summer before the weather heats up as it's best eaten warm from the oven with a good dollop of thick cream.

20 g unsalted butter

castor sugar

400 g cherries

200 g unbleached plain flour

½ teaspoon baking powder

1 pinch salt

300 ml milk

300 ml cream

6 free-range eggs

1 teaspoon pure vanilla extract

icing sugar

Preheat the oven to 200°C. Melt the butter, then brush a shallow ceramic or glass baking dish with this and sprinkle over 1 tablespoon castor sugar to coat evenly. Wash the cherries, then remove the stalks and set aside (I leave the stones in – removing them means you lose juice).

Sift the flour, baking powder and salt into the bowl of an electric mixer, then add 300 g castor sugar. Whisk the milk, cream, eggs and vanilla extract in another bowl, then, with the mixer running at medium speed, slowly pour the milk mixture into the flour to make a smooth batter.

Arrange the cherries over the base of the prepared dish and pour over the batter. Bake for 20–30 minutes until golden and set. Dust with icing sugar and serve immediately. **Serves 10–12**

half the quantity This recipe can simply be halved if you are feeding fewer people, as we did for the dish photographed here.

Summer Pudding

This pudding represents the essence of summer to me, and is high on my comfort-food barometer while still having a touch of class.

Take the trouble to choose the ripest, darkest berries you can find, and dip your bread thoroughly in the juices.

350 ml red wine

240 g castor sugar

1 punnet blackberries

1 punnet raspberries

double cream

pudding

425 g blackberries

200 g raspberries

100 g castor sugar

1 loaf sliced white bread

(sandwich thickness)

To begin making the pudding, put the blackberries and raspberries into a non-reactive saucepan and add the castor sugar. Bring to a gentle simmer and cook for no more than 2 minutes. Remove the pan from the heat and allow to cool.

Choose a mould for your pudding – it needs to be a large, deep dish or jelly mould, although summer pudding can even be made in individual dishes (tea cups work well). Remove the crusts from the bread and cut the bread into shapes that suit your chosen mould, if necessary (the bowl I use is star shaped and I have to angle the slices to fit).

Dip the slices of bread in the berry juices in the saucepan and line the mould, starting with the base and making sure the edges overlap. Spoon the berries and the syrup into the middle of the mould and place a lid of bread on top. Cover the mould well with a doubled layer of plastic film and then thick brown paper or foil tied with string. Weigh the pudding down with a heavy object and refrigerate overnight.

Next day, bring the wine and castor sugar to a boil in a non-reactive saucepan and reduce until syrupy. Add the punnets of blackberries and raspberries and stir very gently to mix. Remove the pan from the heat and allow to cool.

To serve, take the weight and wrappings from the pudding and carefully run a knife around the edge of the mould. Tap the base to release the pudding and invert it onto a plate deep enough to hold the extra syrup. Spoon the syrup and berries over the pudding and serve with double cream.

Serves 6–8

Mince Tartlets

When discussing mince pies, my editor recommended a pastry from the December 1995 edition of *Australian Gourmet Traveller* – it is to die for and perfect when used to make these tiny tarts as it is very short yet holds together well. My fruit mince is on the bittersweet side, the use of cumquats and verjuice providing a great balance to the sweetness of the fruit.

60 g flaked almonds

3 Granny Smith apples

⅓ cup verjuice

200 g seedless raisins

200 g dried apricots

100 g dried figs

200 g sultanas

250 g currants

150 g dried cumquat slices

100 g mixed peel

1 orange

1 lemon

200 g soft light-brown sugar

2 tablespoons honey

2 teaspoons mixed spice

1 teaspoon freshly grated
 nutmeg

150 ml cumquat liqueur

175 g unsalted butter

tartlet pastry

150 g chilled unsalted butter

225 g unbleached plain flour

75 g self-raising flour

55 g icing sugar

1 free-range egg yolk

2½ tablespoons iced water

Preheat the oven to 220°C. Roast the almonds on a baking tray for about 5 minutes, shaking the tray to prevent the nuts from burning. Allow to cool, then chop.

Peel and coarsely grate the apples, then cover with verjuice to prevent discoloration. Chop the raisins, apricots and figs. Combine these in a glass or ceramic bowl with the apple and remaining ingredients, except the butter, and mix thoroughly. Cover with plastic film and leave at room temperature for 24 hours, stirring occasionally. Next day, melt the butter and stir it through the fruit mince.

To make the pastry, dice the chilled butter. Blend the flours, icing sugar and diced butter in a food processor until well combined and the mixture resembles breadcrumbs. Add the egg yolk and iced water and, using the pulse button, process until the mixture starts to come together. Shape the pastry into a disc, then wrap it in plastic film and refrigerate for 1 hour.

Preheat the oven to 210°C. Roll out the pastry until 3 mm thick on a lightly floured bench. Cut rounds of pastry to line the moulds you are using, then cut a corresponding number of lids (I make 36 tiny tarts in mini-muffin trays). Line the moulds with pastry, then add a spoonful of fruit mince and top with a lid, pressing down on the edges to seal the tarts. Make a small cross in the top of each tart with the point of a knife. Bake for 12 minutes, then allow to cool in the trays. (If you are using larger moulds, you will have to bake the tarts for a longer time – the pastry should be golden brown.)

dried cumquats   Noel and Ian Tolley have extensive citrus orchards in the Riverland and, like all smart primary producers, realise the merit of value-adding. Noel produces glacé whole cumquats and dried cumquat slices – I love using the former in desserts and the latter as I've done here or in stocks for poultry or venison dishes.

cumquat liqueur   I've added a twist by using cumquat liqueur here, but brandy does just as well.

Apricot and Brioche Bread-and-butter Pudding

We developed this very rich version of bread-and-butter pudding hoping to release it commercially from our export kitchen. Luscious as it was, the sums didn't add up. However, it's well worth the expense of making it at home. If making brioche seems daunting, buy a panettone from an Italian deli instead and toast it before cutting it into cubes.

2 tablespoons almonds

softened unsalted butter

125 g dried apricots

120 g Brioche (page 145)

900 ml milk

600 ml cream

8 free-range eggs

125 g castor sugar

Preheat the oven to 220°C. Roast the almonds on a baking tray for about 5 minutes, shaking the tray to prevent the nuts from burning. Allow to cool, then roughly chop. Reduce the oven temperature to 200°C.

Grease a deep, large ovenproof bowl with 1 tablespoon softened butter. Slice the apricots and cut the brioche into large cubes. Arrange some apricots over the base of the bowl, then cover this with a layer of brioche cubes. Sprinkle over the chopped almonds, then add another layer of apricots and brioche cubes and finally add a few pieces of apricots to the top.

Heat the milk and cream in a saucepan. Whisk the eggs and castor sugar together, then pour in the hot milk mixture and stir to combine. Pour this custard over the apricot and brioche layers and dot the top with a little butter. Bake for 30–35 minutes until the custard has set. Cool slightly before serving. **Serves 6**

reconstituting apricots   If your dried apricots aren't moist, you may need to reconstitute them – try using a little verjuice for this.

Christmas Cake

I have always had problems stopping the outside of my Christmas cakes from scorching. Even using four layers of paper didn't quite do the trick. Then Timara, a young friend helping me, said that her grandmother used cardboard instead of paper. We followed suit and for good measure added a dish of water to the shelf below the cake to help prevent it from drying out – success!

500 g sultanas

300 g currants

175 g seedless raisins

150 g dried cumquat slices *or*

¼ cup good-quality bitter

marmalade

150 g mixed peel

grated zest of 2 oranges

120 ml brandy

300 g unbleached plain flour

½ teaspoon freshly grated

nutmeg

½ teaspoon ground mixed spice

½ teaspoon salt

220 g softened unsalted butter

200 g soft light-brown sugar

4 large free-range eggs

100 g blanched almonds

Put all the dried fruit and the orange zest into a large non-reactive bowl and mix thoroughly, then pour in the brandy and mix again. Leave for 24 hours at room temperature, turning the mixture once or twice to distribute the brandy evenly.

Preheat the oven to 140°C and grease a 24 cm round cake tin. Flatten out a cardboard box and cut a round to fit the base of the cake tin, then cut strips to line the sides. Position these in the tin, then add a baking-paper lining, making sure the paper comes 10 cm above the rim of the tin. Sift the flour, spices and salt into a large bowl.

Using an electric mixer, cream the butter and brown sugar until pale and thick and the sugar has dissolved. Beat the eggs in a separate bowl, then slowly mix a tablespoon at a time into the creamed mixture – *do not* hurry this process as the mixture curdles easily. When all the egg has been incorporated, fold in the spiced flour very gently, then fold in the dried fruit mixture.

Tip the batter into the prepared cake tin and smooth the top. Make a pattern over the surface of the cake with the blanched almonds and bake for 3 hours. (Standing a baking dish of water on the shelf below will help ensure the cooked cake is moist.) Insert a skewer into the middle of the cake – if it comes out clean, the cake is cooked. It may, however, need up to another 20 minutes.

Allow the cake to cool in the tin for 30 minutes before transferring it to a wire rack to cool completely. Wrap the cooled cake in a doubled layer of baking or greaseproof paper and then in a doubled layer of foil and store in an airtight tin.

blanched almonds   To blanch almonds, pour boiling water over the nuts and leave them for a few minutes for the skins to soften, then slip off the skins with your fingers.

Christmas Pudding with Brandy Butter

My Christmas pudding has an interesting point of difference – it is so heavy with Barossa dried fruit that it needs no sugar at all. Rather than suet, which I love but which makes this pudding far too dense, I use butter, which means leftovers make the moistest cake imaginable. The brandy butter is based on a recipe from my editor's mother – the cumquat brandy is my touch.

115 g candied citron peel

250 g mixed peel

225 g currants

225 g seedless raisins

225 g sultanas

75 g flaked almonds

300 ml port

115 g unbleached plain flour

1 good pinch ground cinnamon

1 good pinch freshly grated
 nutmeg

1 good pinch ground ginger

1 good pinch ground mace

1 teaspoon salt

225 g chilled unsalted butter

225 g fresh breadcrumbs

3 free-range eggs

brandy butter

175 g icing sugar

175 g softened unsalted butter

6 tablespoons cumquat brandy
 or 8 tablespoons brandy

Chop the citron peel, then combine it with the mixed peel, dried fruit, almonds and port in a large non-reactive bowl and mix thoroughly. Cover with plastic film and leave at room temperature for 24 hours, stirring several times.

Sift the flour, spices and salt into a large bowl, then grate in the butter coarsely. Stir in the breadcrumbs and add the fruit mixture. Whisk the eggs until light and frothy and stir through the pudding mixture until well combined.

Dust a 30 cm square of calico with a little flour, then spoon the pudding mixture into the middle. Gather up the cloth and tie it securely with string at the top of the pudding. Steam the pudding in a large double steamer or boil in a large saucepan for 6 hours, replenishing the water every 30 minutes or as necessary. Suspend the boiled pudding in a cool, airy place to mature before using – I make ours in October. (Christmas puddings certainly mature with standing, but the main issues are having the right balance of flavours in the first place and ensuring a long cooking time. Puddings can become mouldy if the weather is humid or if several are hung too close together, so if you don't have time to mature your pudding, or the weather is against you, it won't matter as long as the balance is fine.)

Make the brandy butter on Christmas morning (it can be made the day before but it needs to be wrapped really well to avoid it becoming tainted in the refrigerator). Cream the icing sugar and butter in an electric mixer until white, thick and fluffy and the sugar has dissolved. This takes some time, so be patient. Slowly beat in the brandy, a teaspoonful at a time, tasting as you go. Cover with plastic film and refrigerate.

To serve, steam the pudding in its cloth in the top of a steamer or double saucepan for 1 hour or until heated through. Meanwhile, let the brandy butter stand at room temperature for 20 minutes, then transfer it to 2 serving bowls.

This pudding makes wonderful eating cold as cake if you have leftovers! Serves 20

two puddings   You can also make this pudding as 2 smaller ones to serve 16. Just divide the mixture in half and wrap each in calico, then steam or boil as above in separate pots.

summerautumnwinterspring

A Vintage Picnic Picnics have long been part of life in the Barossa. I have a large black-and-white print of a photograph of a nineteenth-century picnic in full swing on river flats somewhere in the Valley. Some twenty people, all dressed in their best and with a glass in their hand, are gathered around a huge dray piled high with baskets overflowing with food and wine. Children play games nearby, and a beast is being cooked over a fire.

This photograph appeared in the local paper two decades ago as part of a feature about the Barossa Vintage Festival. I was so taken with it that I bought a reprint, deciding then and there to recreate such a picnic on the river flat at the Pheasant Farm. Tucked away in the lee of the cliff, this flat includes pear trees from a defunct orchard and has views over the river of large gums and rows and rows of grapevines. A large dray, pulled not by horses as in the original, but by Col's tractor, became our table, and simple picnic fare was laid out for everyone to share. We dug a pit for roasting, and positioned logs around it on which people could sit. This was when our children were small, and they and their friends spent the afternoon rolling down the sandy cliff that sheltered us. I remember these idyllic days starting at lunchtime and going on into the night, the cooking pit keeping us warm as the air grew chilly.

Our lives seem so much more pressured these days, but we still like to picnic when we can. Picnics are an autumn pursuit for us. Summer is out, simply because of the threat of snakes, while winter is for lazy afternoons by the open fire. And in spring we're far too busy reacting to the changes in the garden and vineyard to have time for languid lunches. Autumn always seems to arrive just in the nick of time in the Valley. Our summers are long and hot, and by March things are usually getting frantic as we head into vintage. Then suddenly the searing heat gives way and the first of the cool autumn air arrives. I find this weather so invigorating – with vintage tailing off and the last of the produce from the orchard and garden ready for preserving, the pressure eases noticeably and I start to feel revitalised after the long, hot spell.

By happy coincidence, autumn is also the time for wild mushrooms. If the early rains have been, we often venture out to our most favourite picnic spots of all – in the pine forests of Mount Crawford or near Heggie's vineyards behind Angaston – in the hope of coming home with some bounty. We always go well prepared but without excess gear, knowing that once we've eaten we'll have an empty basket to fill with mushrooms before heading home. We can't be too heavily laden as we also have to negotiate a few fences en route! Getting to secret picnic sites is half the fun of the exercise, I always think.

A rug is the one item we never forget, as autumn in the Valley can be pretty chilly. As for the food, there's nothing I like better on a picnic than a freshly

baked chicken pie (page 127) – it's a meal in itself and you can eat it in your hands, which means no plates to carry in and out. A pot of just-made green tomato chutney (page 102) is perfect to take for the pies. It's great at 'forest' temperature rather than hot from the stove or cold from the fridge, as is a fresh and rustic tomato soup (page 106). If I'm really organised, I may strain some cow's or goat's curd the night before and then stud it with verjuice-soaked sultanas (page 105) to serve with fresh pears. All else that is needed is a loaf of wood-fired bread from Apex, our champion bakery in Tanunda, some salad leaves, extra-virgin olive oil and vinegar from the kitchen table, a pepper grinder and a pot of sea salt. Oh, and some wine and a bottle opener, of course.

On first entering the forest I always feel as though I'm walking on a cloud – the bed of pine needles mutes all sounds and cushions your tread, a strange sensation. Shards of light slant through the closely planted trees, and I find once in the forest I can't help but scan the shadows constantly for a glimpse of a mushroom cap pushing its way through the needles. Slippery jacks (*Suillus granulatus*) are common near us, and I always look for young, firm ones, rejecting those that are old and spongy. Any we do find are cut close to the ground and arranged on a cloth in our empty picnic basket in a single layer, so the dirt doesn't travel from one to another. And then it's home for another feast!

Green Tomato Chutney

Chutneys may be old-fashioned to some, but I'm never without them, whether to serve with cold meat or to add to a curry. This chutney (see opposite) is excellent with the chicken pies we take on picnics (page 127). In fact, I love the flavour of green tomatoes so much, particularly when teamed with sultanas as here, that I'm making a green tomato pasta sauce commercially, using Sicilian flavours.

1 kg green tomatoes

3 Granny Smith apples

3 onions

3 cloves garlic

600 ml white-wine vinegar

250 g sultanas

1 teaspoon salt

1 teaspoon freshly ground
  black pepper

175 g soft brown sugar

Core the green tomatoes and apples, then peel the apples. Roughly chop the tomatoes, apples and onions, then finely chop the garlic.

Put half the vinegar and the remaining ingredients into a non-reactive pot and bring to a boil. Reduce to a simmer and cook gently for 40 minutes.

Add the remaining vinegar and simmer for a further 20 minutes until the chutney thickens. Check for seasoning and ladle into warm, sterilised jars. Seal, then invert the jars to create a vacuum. **Makes 1.25 litres**

Grape Mustard

I am always on the lookout for ways to use our grapes. I first saw a version of this mustard in France and loved it for its rich colour, let alone its flavour. I've been making it ever since and have found the trick is to use both the juice and a good red-wine vinegar. It's fabulous with rabbit dishes, by the way.

250 g yellow mustard seeds

400 ml black grape juice

250 ml red-wine vinegar

2 tablespoons good-quality
  thick honey

Soak the mustard seeds in the grape juice and vinegar overnight. Purée this mixture in a food processor or blender until well homogenised. Add the honey to combine. Spoon into warm, sterilised jars and seal, then invert the jars to create a vacuum. **Makes 900 ml**

Fig and Prune Mustard

I first read about this type of mustard in Madeleine Kamman's *In Madeleine's Kitchen* and then later in Patricia Wells' *At Home in Provence*. Considering the Barossa is 'prune country', and prunes and figs in all forms appeal, I now make this year-round. It is so versatile it can be eaten with Rillettes (page 66), a poached chook or a lamb chop, the vinegar providing that sweet–sour edge I love so much.

400 g dried figs

400 g pitted prunes

300 ml red-wine vinegar

2 cinnamon sticks

125 ml grainy mustard

Finely chop the figs and prunes. Bring the vinegar, cinnamon sticks and dried fruit to a gentle simmer in a non-reactive saucepan and cook until the fruit is soft.

Remove the cinnamon sticks and blend the mixture to a coarse texture in a food processor, then fold in the mustard. Spoon into warm, sterilised jars and seal with screw-top lids, then invert the jars to create a vacuum. **Makes 1.5 litres**

Fig, Prune and Red-wine Mustard

This is a variation of the mustard above, but as red wine is used rather than red-wine vinegar, the flavour is softer.

400 g dried figs

400 g pitted prunes

250 ml red wine

1/3 cup red-wine vinegar

1/2 teaspoon quatre épices

200 g grainy mustard

finely grated zest of 1 lemon

Finely chop the figs and prunes. Bring the wine, vinegar, quatre épices and the dried fruit to a gentle simmer in a non-reactive saucepan and cook until the fruit is soft.

Blend the mixture to a coarse texture in a food processor, then fold in the mustard and lemon zest. Spoon into warm, sterilised jars and seal with screw-top lids, then invert the jars to create a vacuum. **Makes 1.5 litres**

Bruschetta with Cavolo Nero

I had bruschetta with cavolo nero at Cantinetta Antinori in Florence when lunching with my friend Ann Parronchi. I so loved the simplicity of it that I brought seeds for this exquisite dark cabbage home with me (all above board, I assure you). The olive oil that finished the dish at our lunch was the secret ingredient – it was the first crush of the season at its challenging best.

1 kg cavolo nero

1 litre chicken stock

new season's extra-virgin
  olive oil

4 slices wood-fired bread

1 clove garlic

sea salt

freshly ground black pepper

Remember – each ingredient used here *must* be perfect!

Go through the cavolo nero, choosing leaves of a similar size and rejecting any larger, older ones. Wash the leaves, leaving them whole, then bunch them together. Bring the stock to a simmer in a large saucepan and simmer the cavolo nero until tender, about 45 minutes. Strain the leaves, then moisten them with a little olive oil and keep warm.

Toast the bread, then rub with the cut garlic clove while still warm. Dip the toast quickly into the cooking liquor, then put each slice onto a serving plate. Divide the cavolo nero between the slices of toast, then season with salt and drizzle generously with the olive oil. Add a grinding of pepper and serve with more oil in a jug alongside. **Serves 4**

Fresh Curd Studded with Verjuice-soaked Sultanas

A couple of years ago I was walking through Paris with Stephanie Alexander, exploring the food shops and stalls, when I saw a ball of cheese similar to the one on page 100. I immediately thought how perfect the idea was for the Barossa. With the Kernich family dairy setting up their own farmhouse cheese factory (see pages 316–19), we might even be able to make this a regional speciality.

80 g sultanas

125 ml verjuice

1 teaspoon salt

500 g fresh Jersey *or*
  goat's curd

Soak the sultanas in the verjuice overnight. Meanwhile, stir the salt into the curd and tip it into the centre of a large square of clean muslin. Gather up the corners and tie them with a piece of string. Hang the curd over a bowl in the refrigerator or a cool place overnight to collect the whey.

When you are ready to serve, mound the cheese on a plate, then press the sultanas over the surface. Serve with dried biscuits or sliced pear alongside to scoop up the cheese. **Makes 500 g mouthfuls**   If you let the curd drain for at least 1½ days, you can then mould it into small balls, which you then roll in the sultanas. These are great to serve with drinks.

White Gazpacho with Sultana Grapes

This soup (see opposite) is based on a traditional dish from a Spanish wine-producing region, and is yet again a way I've found of using our grapes during harvest. The verjuice is my addition because I have it to hand. You don't have to be as extravagant – use a mixture of verjuice and water, if you like, or purée seedless grapes and use that juice. Let your tastebuds be your guide.

150 g blanched almonds

4 thick slices good white bread

cold water

2 cloves garlic

salt

150 ml extra-virgin olive oil

600 ml verjuice

1 large bunch sultana grapes

Finely grind the almonds in a food processor. Remove the crusts from the bread, then cover the bread with water and leave to soak for 10 minutes. Drain the bread, then squeeze out as much water as possible. Mince the garlic and then cream it with 1 teaspoon salt by dragging the back of a large knife over it a number of times.

In a food processor, blend the ground almonds, soaked bread, creamed garlic and olive oil. Gradually pour in the verjuice and adjust the consistency of the soup with about 250 ml cold water. Season with salt and chill. Serve in chilled soup dishes with sultana grapes scattered over the surface. **Serves 4**

Fresh Tomato and Basil Soup

This began with Richard Olney's Grape Harvesters' Soup from his *Simple French Food* – I was initially attracted by the name and in fact used to make it for our own pickers. This rustic soup is almost a stew (it can be thinned with a little good stock, if you like), and is just as delicious served at room temperature, so is perfect for a picnic.

2 kg very ripe, vine-ripened
  tomatoes

5 large onions

4 cloves garlic

extra-virgin olive oil

sea salt

freshly ground black pepper

1 cup finely chopped
  fresh basil

Roughly chop the tomatoes and onions, and finely chop the garlic. In a large pot, gently fry the onion in $1/4$ cup olive oil until soft. Add the tomato and cook gently until soft and juicy. Season with salt and pepper and stir in the chopped basil.

Just before serving, drizzle a little olive oil over the surface of the soup. **Serves 6**

a meal on its own For a complete meal, add a chunk of bread to the bowl and moisten it with extra-virgin olive oil before pouring in the soup.

Potato with Boletus Mushrooms

The earthy flavours of potatoes and boletus mushrooms combine fantastically. This dish tastes even better if you've gathered your own mushrooms (provided you've had expert tuition about what's safe to pick). If that's so, and you have some left over, rather than refrigerate them try drying them for later use, as the flavour of boletus intensifies with age. A small kitchen dehydrator is perfect for the job.

4 × 10 cm wide boletus
  mushrooms
500 g waxy potatoes
extra-virgin olive oil
2 sprigs thyme
2 sprigs oregano
2 shallots (optional)
75 g unsalted butter
basil *or* thyme
sea salt
freshly ground black pepper

Preheat the oven to 230°C. Wipe the mushroom caps with a lightly oiled paper towel, then slice each mushroom into 1 cm wide strips. Set aside. Wash but don't peel the potatoes, then cut them into 5 mm thick slices.

Choose a large, shallow baking dish and toss the potato with enough olive oil to coat it, then strip the leaves from the thyme and sprinkle these over the potato. Spread the potato evenly over the dish, making sure that as many slices as possible make contact with the base so that they caramelise during cooking, then bake for about 10 minutes. Turn over the slices and cook for a further 10 minutes until both sides are golden. You'll need to keep an eye on the potato as different varieties cook at different rates: if it colours too quickly, turn the oven down to 200°C.

Meanwhile, chop the oregano leaves to yield 1 tablespoon, and finely chop the shallots. Cook a knob of butter in a non-reactive frying pan with the shallots, if using, until nut-brown, then add a splash of olive oil to inhibit burning. Add half the mushrooms, then season with salt and pepper. Transfer to a warm plate and cook the remaining mushrooms. Add the oregano and check the seasoning, then let the mushrooms sit (lots of delicious juices will accumulate, so choose a plate with a lip). Toss the juicy mushrooms with the golden potato and serve with grilled veal chops and a green salad. **Serves 4**

Witlof, Watercress, Bocconcini, Walnut and Grape Salad

Walnut oil has a very short shelf-life – it oxidises and becomes rancid very quickly. It makes sense, then, to buy it from a reputable handler, one whose shop has a fast turnover, and to store it in the refrigerator.

100 g walnuts

2 red witlof

1 small handful watercress

1 small handful salad burnet

1 small handful red grapes

1 lemon

extra-virgin olive oil

4 bocconcini

1 tablespoon roughly chopped
 lemon thyme

caper vinaigrette

⅓ cup walnut oil

1 tablespoon verjuice

1 tablespoon capers

freshly ground black pepper

Preheat the oven to 220°C. Roast the walnuts on a baking tray for about 5 minutes until beginning to brown, shaking the trays to prevent the nuts from burning. If they are not fresh season's, rub the walnuts in a clean tea towel to remove the bitter skins. Put the nuts into a coarse sieve and shake away the skins. Allow to cool.

Separate the witlof leaves, then wash and dry carefully with the watercress and salad burnet. Cut the grapes in half and remove the seeds. Toss the salad leaves in a large bowl, then divide them between 4 plates. Slice the lemon finely and cut these slices into small pieces, then mix with the grapes and roasted walnuts and scatter over the salad. Pour a little extra-virgin olive oil over the bocconcini, then roll these in the lemon thyme. Slice thinly and add to the salad leaves.

To make the vinaigrette, whisk the walnut oil and verjuice until amalgamated, then add the capers and pepper. Dress the salad just before serving. **Serves 4**

preparing in advance   The bocconcini can be dressed with the olive oil and lemon thyme up to a day before serving; however, the lemon thyme will become black and unpalatable if this is done too far ahead.

Slow-cooked Cannellini Beans

I became hooked on the fresh cannellini beans we had in Italy, and now love the dried beans cooked the same way. Soaking them overnight is essential, though, as is using a first-rate oil – its flavour permeates the beans. If you do not want to use the amount of olive oil listed here, you can use two-thirds chicken stock and a third oil, if you like. But guess which version I prefer!

375 g cannellini beans

1 quorm garlic

500 ml good-quality extra-
 virgin olive oil

2 sprigs thyme

4 fresh bay leaves

2 slices prosciutto

Soak the cannellini beans overnight in a large pot of water – the water should come at least 5 cm above the beans.

Preheat the oven to 200°C. Trim the top from the garlic, then rub the quorm with a little of the olive oil and roast for 35–40 minutes until soft and caramelised. Set aside.

Drain the beans, then put them into a large pot and add fresh water to come 5 cm above the beans. Bring to a boil and simmer for 1 hour, then drain well. Transfer the beans to a terracotta or cast-iron pot with a lid. Pour the olive oil over the beans and add the thyme and bay leaves. Squeeze the garlic cloves carefully from the quorm and tear the prosciutto into small pieces and add both to the beans. Stand the pot on a simmer mat and heat very gently. Cook the beans overnight on as low a heat as possible, with a bubble rising to the surface occasionally. Serve warm or at room temperature. Serves 4–6

Warm Chickpea, Fennel and Parsley Salad

When the first of the fennel comes through it's time to celebrate. I could hardly bear to unpack the case delivered to the door for our photo shoot, so beautiful were these plump specimens! For some reason I always feel virtuous when I make this salad for lunch: it's fresh, tasty, filling and healthy and it fits the bill when I limit myself to taking a short break at the office.

375 g dried chick peas

water

1 large brown onion

12 large sprigs thyme

1 teaspoon salt

1 small red onion

2 small sticks celery

1 small fennel bulb

1 large handful flat-leaf parsley

garlic vinaigrette

2 cloves garlic

1 teaspoon salt

2 tablespoons red-wine vinegar

160 ml extra-virgin olive oil

Soak the chick peas overnight in a large pot of water – the water should come at least 5 cm above the peas.

Drain the chick peas and put them into a fresh pot of water. Peel and quarter the brown onion and add it to the pot with the thyme tied into a bundle. Bring the pot to a boil, then turn the heat down to a simmer and cook slowly for about $1\frac{1}{2}$ hours. Just before the chick peas are cooked, add the salt (if added earlier, it will inhibit the cooking process as it toughens the chick peas). When they are ready, the chick peas should melt in your mouth but still retain their shape when stirred. Drain the chick peas and discard the thyme and onion.

Finely dice the red onion, celery and fennel. Pluck the leaves from the parsley to yield 1 cup, discarding the stalks, and toss through the warm chick peas with the chopped vegetables.

To make the vinaigrette, mince the garlic and then cream it with the salt by dragging the back of a large knife over it a number of times. Whisk the vinegar, olive oil and creamed garlic until amalgamated, then dress the salad while the chick peas are still warm. Serves 8

Stuffed Baby Capsicums on Olive-bread Croutons with Rocket

This dish is a recreation of an amazing experience I had in a Spanish restaurant – in Tokyo. Prepared by the delicate hand of a Japanese chef using the gutsy flavours of Spain, it was exquisite. There was something very special about the tiny capsicums used – they were no more than 5 cm long! While I'm yet to find fruit of a similar size, this works well with capsicums large and small.

8 baby red capsicums

extra-virgin olive oil

8 super-fine slices of Olive
  and Rosemary Bread
  (page 144)

1 free-range egg yolk

1 teaspoon lemon juice

2 hardboiled free-range
  egg yolks

1 × 140 g can tuna in olive oil

sea salt

freshly ground black pepper

4 small handfuls young
  rocket leaves

Preheat the oven to 220°C. Carefully cut away the top of each capsicum with a paring knife (the tops are later used as lids) and remove the seeds and ribs. Brush both the lids and the cleaned capsicums with olive oil and roast on a baking tray for 20 minutes. Allow to cool slightly, then peel away the skin from each capsicum, taking care not to tear the flesh. Set the capsicums and lids aside to cool to room temperature, then refrigerate until chilled.

Meanwhile, reduce the oven temperature to 200°C. Brush the slices of olive bread with a little olive oil and toast in the oven until golden, about 20 minutes. Set aside.

Make a rich mayonnaise by whisking the egg yolk with the lemon juice and then slowly whisking in 250 ml olive oil. Start by adding the oil drop by drop and then in a slow but steady stream, until the mixture is thick and glossy (for more about making mayonnaise, turn to page 20). Mash the hardboiled yolks with a fork and drain the tuna well, then fold both through the mayonnaise. Season with salt and pepper and refrigerate until chilled.

Just before serving, carefully fill the roasted capsicums with the tuna mayonnaise and replace the 'lids'. Arrange a few washed and dried rocket leaves on each plate and drizzle over a little olive oil. Place a filled capsicum on an olive-bread crouton and serve on the rocket. (One capsicum makes a great starter, while two can be served as a main course.) Makes 8

The Vineyard

We knew nothing about grapevines when we bought our original vineyard, of which the Pheasant Farm is a part, in 1973, but we learnt quickly and happily embraced the tradition of celebrating vintage.

As newcomers, we were lucky to secure the services of a few local 'gun' pickers, the rest of our crew being made up of people on working holidays – everyone from lawyers, accountants, nurses and students to very fit retirees. Colin was bucket carrier and drove the loaded truck to the weighbridge, where there would often be delays, so much so that I would frequently find myself taking dinner down to him. He didn't seem to mind, as there was never a shortage of characters with whom to swap Valley stories and share a 'schlook' while waiting in the queue.

I used to take food and drink out to the pickers, too, but that tradition waned as I became busier. I made it up at the end of each vintage by cooking a great feast for everyone instead. Sometimes we took all our pickers to Die Galerie restaurant in Tanunda, where a whole pig would be baked in the wood-fired oven. Another year we took them to the concert put on as part of the Barossa Vintage Festival, held every second Easter, where they sang and danced into the wee hours with a thousand others (just as well we'd finished picking!).

Now, however, most of the Valley's grapes are mechanically harvested. It's a far less personal method, but the spirit of the occasion is still there – the end of the season is in sight, after all. Going mechanical was inevitable, I guess, as handpicking is comparatively costly and finding pickers has become increasingly difficult. The good locals are getting older and find it tough in the heat, and their children are more likely to be at university or getting on with their careers than picking grapes. But some small vineyards will always use

pickers, and some tender varieties will always need to be handpicked, so we will never lose the tradition completely. Thankfully we still get young backpackers, particularly from Europe, who love the job and seem to revel in our heat.

The first sign that handpicking is in progress is the sudden appearance of lines of cars on the side of the road, away from any houses or farm buildings. You'll see hats or headscarves bobbing up and down between the vines, and, if you stop, you'll hear people calling out to one another: a good gang is a happy gang. Most of all, you'll notice dusty, dirty and often scantily clad young people buying supplies in the local co-op at the end of the day. You can tell these are the visitors, as the locals are covered from head to toe to keep the sun out!

When vintage is in full swing, traffic in the Valley is held up as tractors pulling grape bins bring the average speed down.

No one seems to mind the inconvenience. Old trucks, registered for these few weeks of the year, are a little quicker – but I have no doubt they'd be retired if not for this annual stint.

Once the grapes are in the winery, the activity intensifies, especially at Rockford, where a traditional basket press is still used (see opposite). A hands-on affair that requires great stamina, the crush here reminds Col of his days shovelling grapes by the tonne during our first vintage in the Valley. But while we might feel nostalgic about this process, there's nothing romantic about aching backs and arms.

Permeating all this activity is the smell of vintage – the sweet stickiness of just-picked grapes through to the heavy, overpowering aroma of the start of ferment. Some visitors can't abide it, but for me it's the indication that we've come full circle. And that's something to celebrate.

Rags of Fresh Pasta with Roasted Pumpkin, Pancetta and Sage

Pumpkins may be available to us year-round, but they're not picked until after vintage in the Barossa. My mother gave me my first lesson in choosing a good pumpkin when I was seven; the subject was a Queensland blue – I was to look for deep-ochre flesh and a thin, dark-green line under the skin. Today, pumpkin is my sentimental favourite, particularly if it's been roasted the way I give here.

450 g peeled pumpkin chunks

extra-virgin olive oil

6 thin slices rolled pancetta

16 sage leaves

50 g softened unsalted butter

salt

freshly ground black pepper

150 g freshly shaved
  Parmigiano-Reggiano

fresh pasta

500 g unbleached strong flour

4 × 61 g free-range eggs

1 free-range egg yolk (optional)

To make the pasta, tip the flour onto a workbench and make a well in the centre. Whisk the eggs and tip them into the well, then incorporate them into the flour using a pastry scraper. You may need to add an extra yolk if the dough is too dry. Knead the dough by hand until it is shiny and firm to the touch, about 10 minutes (you can also do this in an electric mixer fitted with a dough hook, in which case it will take 5–8 minutes). Form the dough into a ball, then wrap it in plastic film and refrigerate for 30 minutes.

Meanwhile, preheat the oven to 200°C. Brush the pumpkin with extra-virgin olive oil and bake on a baking tray for 25 minutes. Crisp the pancetta and the sage leaves, dotted with the butter, on separate baking trays for 12 minutes. Keep a close eye on the sage so it doesn't burn.

Using a pasta machine, roll out the rested dough following your machine's instructions. Once you have passed the dough through the finest setting, use a knife to cut the pasta strips into pieces about 5 cm × 4 cm.

To cook, bring a large pot of salted water to a boil and gently slide in the pasta rags. Bring the water back to a boil and cook for 3 minutes or so, stirring the pasta gently to keep it well separated (a tablespoon of olive oil in the water can help prevent sticking).

Drain the cooked pasta well, then toss it with the roasted pumpkin, pancetta and sage. Add a grinding of pepper and serve with the Parmigiano-Reggiano. **Serves 4**

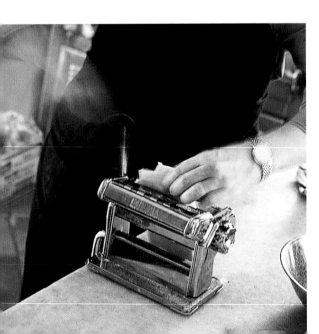

Stinging Nettle Risotto

I first had this dish when Vince Garreffa and his friend John Maiorana invited presenters from the Perth Master Class to Vince's home for what turned out to be an incredible meal. I've since cooked nettle risotto on holidays in Italy and when I've found myself in our vineyard at the right time: stinging nettles grow very, very fast and need to be harvested while young and tender.

young stinging nettles

250 g unsalted butter

1.5–2 litres chicken stock

2 large brown onions

3 cloves garlic

2 sticks celery

extra-virgin olive oil

400 g arborio rice

sea salt

freshly ground black pepper

180 ml fruity white wine

freshly grated Parmigiano-
  Reggiano

Wearing thick rubber gloves, wash the nettles, discarding roots, debris and any older leaves. You need 3 cups tightly packed, cleaned nettles for the risotto. Melt a knob of the butter in a frying pan and cook the nettles for about 2 minutes, then tip them into a food processor and purée. Set aside.

Heat the stock in a saucepan and keep at a gentle simmer. Finely chop the onions and garlic, and finely slice the celery. Melt 150 g of the butter in a heavy-based, non-reactive pot and add a splash of olive oil to inhibit burning. Gently sauté the onion and garlic in the butter and oil until almost translucent, then add the celery and cook for another 5 minutes. Turn up the heat and add the rice, stirring well until it is gleaming. Season.

Pour in the wine and stir until it has evaporated. Add the first ladleful of stock, stirring to incorporate it, then add the puréed nettles. Continue cooking, adding a ladleful of stock as the last is absorbed and stirring all the while. The texture of the risotto is a personal choice, which is why I suggest 1.5–2 litres stock. The rice will take about 20 minutes to cook and shouldn't go beyond being al dente.

Remove the pan from the heat and add the remaining butter to 'velvet' the rice. Check for seasoning and serve with grated Parmigiano-Reggiano alongside. Serves 4

Green Olive Gnocchi with Green Olive Sauce

This is one of my family's comfort foods. The recipe has changed a great deal over the years: I now only make gnocchi with waxy potatoes, and I find that melted butter produces a much lighter result than egg. The sauce has also become lighter, but don't be tempted to leave out the cream to lighten it further: the cream adds an amazing dimension.

unsalted butter

200 g unbleached plain flour

100 g green olives

500 g waxy potatoes

sea salt

freshly ground black pepper

green olive sauce

1 large onion

3 cloves garlic

1 tablespoon extra-virgin

  olive oil

175 ml reduced chicken stock

100 ml cream

100 g green olives

2 tablespoons freshly chopped

  flat-leaf parsley

To make the sauce, finely chop the onion and garlic, then sweat these in the olive oil until softened. Add the stock and cream and cook gently until reduced to your preferred thickness. Set aside. Slice the flesh away from each olive in 4 pieces, then discard the stones. Set aside.

To make the gnocchi, preheat the oven to 100°C and butter a serving dish. Spread the flour out into a rectangle on a bench. Slice the flesh away from each olive in 4 pieces, then discard the stones. Peel the potatoes, then steam them until cooked right through. While still hot, pass them through a potato ricer or food mill so that the potato falls evenly over the flour. Sprinkle sea salt and the sliced olives over the flour and potato.

Melt 50 g unsalted butter and drizzle it evenly over the potato. Work the flour into the potato little by little using a pastry scraper until you have a firm dough. Knead the dough gently for 5 minutes, then divide it into quarters and roll each piece to make a long, thin sausage about 1 cm in diameter. Cut each sausage into 2.5 cm lengths. Put the prepared serving dish into the oven to warm through. Gently warm the sauce and add the olive pieces.

I find a large, heavy-based 6 cm-deep baking dish perfect for poaching gnocchi. Fill such a dish with water, then bring it to a boil and add salt. When the water is boiling, raise the heat and quickly slip in all the gnocchi at once if the dish is large enough to take them in a single layer, then reduce the heat so that the water isn't too turbulent. Allow the gnocchi to cook for 1 minute after they have risen to the surface, then skim them out and put them into the warm serving dish and season. (If your poaching dish is not large enough to take the gnocchi in one layer, you will have to cook them in batches.)

Stir the parsley through the sauce, then toss with the gnocchi, grind on pepper and serve immediately. Serves 4

an alternative   Try cooking 125 g butter until nut-brown, then toss the poached gnocchi in it until crisp. Forego the sauce and finish off the buttery juices with a little lemon juice or verjuice.

Whole Whiting Baked with Wild Fennel, Oregano and Lemon

I revel in baking a whole fish, complete with head, of course. Fish tastes best of all cooked on the bone, and the technique used here means the skin caramelises a little, which is just delicious. Serving a whole fish means everyone is more engaged, too, with what they're eating. This is also an incredibly simple way to get a great meal on the table quickly.

extra-virgin olive oil

4 generous handfuls wild
  fennel *or* 2 handfuls dill

6 × 440 g gutted and scaled
  whiting

½ cup roughly chopped
  oregano

sea salt

freshly ground black pepper

2 lemons

lemon juice

Preheat the oven to 230°C. Brush a large baking dish with olive oil. Arrange half the wild fennel over the base and put the whiting on top. Brush the fish with olive oil, then sprinkle over the oregano and season with salt and pepper. Slice the lemon finely and arrange on top of and inside the whiting.

Bake for 10 minutes. Carefully turn the whiting over and bake for a further 5 minutes. Before serving, sprinkle with a little salt and lemon juice. **Serves 6**

Country Chicken and Mushroom Pies

I'm a bit of a pie-for-all-seasons sort of person. If you're having guests, all the work is done in advance and the uncooked pie waits in the refrigerator until it goes into the oven. And then there's the flourish of presenting it straight from the oven to the table – so clever! These pies are just as great cold on a picnic (see pages 96–101); in fact, the buttery pastry is extra delicious when really chilled.

softened unsalted butter

6 free-range chicken Marylands

sea salt

freshly ground black pepper

450 ml reduced golden
   chicken stock

7 large field mushrooms

¼ cup unbleached plain flour

200 ml cream

2 tablespoons freshly chopped
   herbs (oregano, thyme,
   flat-leaf parsley)

1 free-range egg

¼ cup milk

sour cream pastry

200 g chilled unsalted butter

250 g plain flour

125 ml sour cream

Preheat the oven to 220°C. Butter a baking dish with softened butter, then add the chicken and season with salt and pepper. Roast the chicken for 20 minutes, then allow to rest for 15 minutes. Pick the meat off the bone and chop it roughly.

Meanwhile, heat the stock. Slice the mushrooms and fry in 50 g butter in a large saucepan. Sprinkle the flour over the mushrooms and stir to coat evenly. Gradually pour in the hot stock and cream, stirring to incorporate. Simmer gently until thickened. If too thick, stir in a little extra stock. Fold the chicken meat and herbs through the mushroom mixture and season with salt and pepper. Refrigerate until chilled.

To make the pastry, dice the butter, then pulse with the flour in a food processor until the mixture resembles fine breadcrumbs. Add the sour cream and continue to pulse until the dough starts to incorporate into a ball. Wrap the dough in plastic film and refrigerate for 20 minutes.

Roll the chilled pastry out until 5 mm thick and cut rounds to line 6 individual pie dishes, taking the pastry over the edge of each to form a lip. With the remaining pastry, cut out 6 smaller rounds – these are the pie lids. Fill the pastry cases with the chicken mixture. Whisk the egg and milk together and brush this over the pastry 'lip'. Put the lids into position and press around the edges with a fork to seal. Using a sharp paring knife, trim the pastry and, working from the centre to the edge, decoratively score the top of each lid.

Refrigerate the pies while preheating the oven to 220°C. Brush the tops of the pies with the egg wash again and bake for 20 minutes. Reduce the heat to 180°C and bake for a further 25 minutes. Allow the pies to cool slightly before turning out. Serve hot, cold or chilled with onion confit or Green Tomato Chutney (page 102). **Serves 6**

Warm Salad of Roasted Guinea Fowl, Pomegranate Butter, Sorrel and Caramelised Garlic

Autumn is my favourite food season as it's when guinea fowl and pomegranates, among others, become available, so what better thing to do than bring them together. Game birds have long been a part of our lives – after all, we began farming pheasants back in 1973. Note the short cooking and long resting times here: they're essential if the meat is to be tender and moist.

8 pomegranates

160 g softened unsalted butter

4 quorms garlic

extra-virgin olive oil

2 guinea fowl

24 baby sorrel leaves

16 stems salad burnet

1 lemon

freshly ground black pepper

Cut the pomegranates in half and remove the seeds. Set aside the seeds of 2 pomegranates. Pulse the remaining seeds in a food processor for 15 seconds, then strain the juice through a fine sieve into a non-reactive saucepan. Bring the juice to a boil and reduce by half, which will leave you with about 125 ml. Allow to cool and then chill in the refrigerator.

Pulse the softened butter and reduced pomegranate juice in a food processor until as much juice as possible has amalgamated with the butter. Remove and stir through 1 tablespoon of the reserved pomegranate seeds. Keep at room temperature until required (if making and refrigerating the butter in advance, allow it to come back to room temperature before proceeding).

Meanwhile, preheat the oven to 200°C. Trim the tops from each garlic quorm, then rub the garlic with extra-virgin olive oil and roast for 35–40 minutes until soft and caramelised. Set aside.

Reset the oven to 230°C. Cut away the legs of the guinea fowl and trim the wings back to the first joint. Using your fingers, wedge some pomegranate butter under the skin of each guinea fowl to protect the flesh, and place, breast-side up, in a baking dish that has been brushed with extra-virgin olive oil. Roast for 10 minutes. Turn the guinea fowl over and cook skin-side down for a further 4 minutes. Check the birds are cooked by inserting a skewer into the meatiest part – if the juices run clear or a faint pink, the birds are ready. Remove the guinea fowl from the oven, then turn them over and allow to rest for 8 minutes.

To make the salad, wash and dry the sorrel and salad burnet thoroughly, and trim the salad burnet of its stalks. Remove the zest from the lemon with a lemon zester. Toss the salad leaves with the zest and add a drizzle of extra-virgin olive oil and a grinding of pepper. Carve the guinea fowl breasts off the bone and nestle these in the salad. Gently squeeze the roasted garlic cloves from the quorms and add to the salad with the remaining pomegranate seeds. For a more substantial meal, add quarters of boiled waxy potatoes such as kipflers to the salad. Serves 4

pomegranate stains   Your hands will become stained when removing the seeds from the pomegranates, but lemon juice rubbed into the stains will help.

Roasted Pheasant with Sage, Orange and Juniper Berries

These cooking times are approximate. Translating the time achieved when using a commercial oven to that required by a domestic oven is precariously difficult. Domestic ovens vary greatly in their ability to heat evenly and to recover the heat once the door has been opened. The breast should feel firm and yet yield to a soft squeeze when it is ready.

½ cup loosely packed
  sage leaves

80 g softened unsalted butter

1 × 1 kg pheasant

1 orange

20 juniper berries

2 teaspoons freshly chopped
  marjoram

2 teaspoons freshly chopped
  thyme

125 ml reduced chicken stock

salt

freshly ground black pepper

Preheat the oven to 200°C. Remove the stalks from the sage, if desired, then spread the leaves out on a baking tray and dot with half the butter. Bake for 12 minutes until crisp and nut-brown, then set aside. Increase the oven temperature to 230°C.

Cut the legs away from the pheasant, then cut up either side of the backbone and discard it. 'Spatchcock' the bird by flattening it out. Remove the zest from half the orange with a potato peeler, then juice the orange. Put the pheasant legs and flattened-out breast into a baking dish, skin-side up. Smear the pheasant with the remaining butter, then pour over the orange juice and sprinkle on the juniper berries, marjoram, thyme and zest.

Roast the pheasant for 12 minutes, then reduce the temperature to 180°C and cook for a further 12 minutes. Remove the legs from the baking dish, then turn the breast over and return it to the oven for a further 2 minutes. Check the bird is cooked by inserting a skewer into the meatiest part – if the juices run clear or a faint pint, the bird is ready. Remove from the oven and rest, breast down, for a minimum of 8 minutes. Drain the juices from the baking tray into a small saucepan and add the reduced chicken stock. Bring to a boil and check for seasoning.

Carve the breast away from the bone and serve with the cooked leg, drizzled with the reduced stock and topped with the crisped sage leaves and zest. Serves 2

Roasted Goose with Preserved Lemon and Liver Stuffing and Figs and Caramelised Garlic

Serving goose at Christmas has always been my sentimental favourite, but they're usually a little young for that market, in the Barossa at least. Instead, I find early autumn the ideal time for a plump, mature bird. Oven bags are the perfect medium for this long, slow pot-roasting, where liquid is added continually until the rich meat on the bone is soft to the touch.

5 quorms garlic

extra-virgin olive oil

1 × 2.5 kg goose

125 ml water

50 g unsalted butter

5 large ripe black figs

16 young sage leaves

preserved lemon and liver
  stuffing

4 slices prosciutto

1 small onion

30 g unsalted butter

4 chicken livers

2 pieces preserved lemon

1 tablespoon freshly chopped
  thyme

250 g fresh breadcrumbs

freshly ground black pepper

Preheat the oven to 200°C. Trim the tops from each garlic quorm, then rub the garlic with extra-virgin olive oil and roast for 35–40 minutes until soft and caramelised. Set aside. Increase the oven temperature to 220°C.

To make the stuffing, crisp the prosciutto on a baking tray in the oven, then break it into small pieces. Reduce the oven temperature to 180°C. Chop the onion finely and fry it gently in the butter until softened. Trim the livers of any connective tissue and gently seal in the same pan, then dice. Mince the preserved lemon and combine with the prosciutto, onion, liver, thyme and breadcrumbs. Season with pepper.

Pack the stuffing into the cavity of the goose, then rub the skin with juice from the preserved lemon jar. (This includes the oil from the lemon rind, which helps crisp the skin and give it a delicious flavour.) Put the goose into an oven bag, then put the sealed bag into a deep baking dish. Pour the water into the dish and cook for 1 hour 20 minutes.

Take the goose out of the oven bag and increase the oven temperature to 230°C. Return the goose to the baking dish and roast for a further 20 minutes. Remove from the oven and allow to rest for 25 minutes.

Meanwhile, melt the butter in a saucepan until foaming and nut-brown. Cut the figs in half and cook gently in the butter with the sage leaves for 3 minutes. Serve the roasted goose on a large platter with the figs, sage and roasted garlic to the side. Serves 4

Rabbit and Prune Terrine with Mustard Fruits

Rabbit, wild or farmed, is a hugely underrated meat. It can be tricky to cook – I've seen more overcooked rabbit in my time than just about anything else, and nothing is tougher eating. A terrine avoids this problem altogether, however, and looks a great deal more complicated than it actually is. A great luncheon dish, rabbit and prune terrine is particularly good with sweet–sour mustard fruits.

front and back legs from
  2 × 1.8 kg rabbits
550 g pork back fat
1¼ teaspoons quatre épices
3 teaspoons freshly ground
  black pepper
2 teaspoons salt
¼ cup freshly chopped herbs
  (thyme, sage, parsley)
1 free-range egg
200 g pitted prunes
4 rabbit fillets
mustard fruits

Preheat the oven to 200°C. Bone the rabbit legs, removing as much sinew as possible, then cut the meat into small pieces. You need 575 g boned rabbit meat to proceed. Dice 200 g of the pork back fat, then freeze the remaining fat (this will aid slicing later). Blend the boned rabbit meat, diced back fat, quatre épices, pepper, salt and herbs to a fine texture in a food processor. You may need to do this in batches depending on the strength and size of your machine. Remove to a bowl and incorporate the egg.

Remove the back fat from the freezer and slice it very, very finely. You need enough to line and top 2 terrine moulds. Line the moulds with the back fat, slightly overlapping each slice. Cover the base with a layer of the rabbit mixture, then follow this with a layer of prunes (flatten these slightly before they go in). Remove all sinew from the rabbit fillets, then arrange the fillets on top of the prunes. Add another prune layer and finish with the remaining rabbit mixture. Cover the top of the terrine with the remaining sliced back fat. Put lids on the terrines, then stand them in a baking dish and pour in hot water to come two-thirds of the way up their sides. Make sure that no water is allowed to enter the terrine dish while it is in the water bath. Bake for 45 minutes, then remove the terrines from the water bath and allow them to cool completely before refrigerating.

To serve, run a hot knife around the edge of each terrine and invert onto a serving plate. Slice carefully with a sharp, hot knife. Serve with mustard fruits alongside. **Serves 16**

Thyme-roasted Saddle of Rabbit with Baked Red Onions and Pancetta

This method of cooking a rabbit saddle, complete with liver and kidneys and their fat (which keeps them moist), is a surefire way of making the most of this lovely meat. The only tricky part here is removing the silvery sinew from the saddle – I use a flexible fish-filleting knife for this job.

8 small red onions

1 brown onion

200 g softened unsalted butter

2 tablespoons grainy Dijon
   mustard

1 cup chopped baby sorrel

extra-virgin olive oil

4 large rabbit saddles

2 tablespoons freshly plucked
   lemon thyme leaves

freshly ground black pepper

12 fine slices rolled pancetta

Preheat the oven to 200°C. Cut the base and top away from each red onion, then, with a small paring knife, cut a pocket from the top of each one. Set aside.

Finely chop the brown onion and fry gently in 50 g of the butter until soft, then add the mustard. Set aside. Using a fork, combine the chopped sorrel and 120 g of the butter in a bowl. Set aside.

Brush a baking dish with a little olive oil. Tuck 1 teaspoon of the onion and mustard mixture and 1 teaspoon of the sorrel butter into each prepared red onion. Stand the stuffed onions closely together in the baking dish and bake for 40 minutes until softened but not collapsing. Reset the oven to 220°C.

Remove all sinew from the rabbit saddles, then rub them with olive oil, lemon thyme and pepper. Heat the remaining butter in a frying pan until nut-brown and foaming, then seal the rabbit very gently until pale-golden brown. Transfer to the oven and cook for 12 minutes. Remove the rabbit from the oven, then turn the saddles over and allow them to rest for 8 minutes.

While the rabbit is resting, crisp the pancetta on a baking tray in the oven and warm the baked onions. Serve the rabbit with the crisp pancetta, a baked onion and a dollop of Fig and Prune Mustard (see page 104). Drizzle the pan juices over the rabbit before serving. Serves 4

farmed vs wild rabbits   Farmed rabbits weigh about 1.4 kg each. The saddles from wild rabbits are much smaller, so need less cooking than those from the larger farmed animals.

Braised Pork Neck with Fried Green Tomatoes

Slow-cooking is the perfect process for the less popular but sweetest cuts. If this pork isn't soft to the touch after the specified time, let it go as long as it needs; it won't spoil as long as it cooks slowly. The fried green tomatoes are a special autumn touch – I feel very virtuous knowing I'm wasting nothing in the garden. I love the crunchy coating, and their sweet–sour note cuts the richness of the pork.

1 × 1.65 kg pork neck

¼ cup extra-virgin olive oil

1 tablespoon freshly chopped
  sage

1 tablespoon freshly chopped
  rosemary

1 tablespoon freshly chopped
  oregano

sea salt

freshly ground black pepper

15 g butter

3 red onions

2–3 fresh bay leaves

125 ml verjuice

fried green tomatoes

1 free-range egg

1 tablespoon milk

90 g polenta

90 g unbleached plain flour

6 green tomatoes

50 g butter

¼ cup extra-virgin olive oil

sea salt

freshly ground black pepper

Preheat the oven to 180°C. Rub the pork neck with the olive oil and chopped herbs and season with salt and pepper. In a deep, ovenproof pot (I use a cast-iron cocotte with a tight-fitting lid), seal the pork neck in the butter until lightly golden brown.

Cut the onions into sixths, then put these and the bay leaves to the side of the pork and pour over half the verjuice. Put the lid on the pot, then cook in the oven for 1 hour. Turn the pork over and cook for a further hour.

When the 2 hours' cooking time is up, pour the remaining verjuice over the pork and leave to rest out of the oven for 20 minutes.

Make the fried green tomatoes while the meat is resting. Whisk the egg and milk together and pour into a shallow dish. Put the polenta and flour into separate dishes. Slice the green tomatoes thickly and dust both sides with the flour, then dip into the egg mixture and coat with the polenta. Heat the butter and olive oil in a frying pan, then slip in the tomato slices and fry until golden. Drain on paper towel and season with salt and pepper.

Serve the sliced pork with the fried green tomatoes, boiled potatoes and a bitter green salad.

Serves 6

crockpot   This dish could also be cooked in a crockpot overnight or during the day, so it's ready when you get home.

Pan-fried Lemon and Rosemary Veal Cutlets

How I loved those amazing White Rocks veal chops from Western Australia that used to grace the table at Stephanie's. That extraordinary restaurant is a part of history now, but my memories of sitting at a window table eating that veal have never been surpassed. Thankfully, White Rocks veal is still going strong, and Vince Garreffa of Mondo di Carne, Perth's master butcher, is happy to mail-order.

6 × 2 cm-thick veal cutlets

extra-virgin olive oil

1 tablespoon freshly chopped
  rosemary

¼ teaspoon freshly ground
  black pepper

50 g butter

2 tablespoons lemon juice

Trim the rib bones of all sinew and meat to leave them clean. Rub the olive oil, chopped rosemary and pepper into the veal and leave for 10 minutes for the flavours to infuse.

    Melt the butter in a frying pan until nut-brown and foaming. Pan-fry the cutlets for 6 minutes on the first side, then turn and cook for a further 4 minutes on the other side. Pour the lemon juice into the pan to deglaze it.

    Serve, as shown opposite, with steamed green beans and boiled baby potatoes that have been rolled in melted butter and freshly chopped flat-leaf parsley, or Potato with Boletus Mushrooms (page 110) and a green salad. **Serves 6**

Barbecued Leg of Milk-fed Lamb

I've spoken elsewhere of the wonderful sweetness of milk-fed lamb, but an older leg of lamb will work well here, too, if you adjust the cooking time (double should do it). Using foil to wrap the meat after the initial sealing is optional, but I've found it a boon when entertaining as you can relax with a glass of red instead of having to turn the meat continually.

1 × 1.3 kg leg of milk-fed lamb

2 tablespoons extra-virgin
  olive oil

1½ tablespoons freshly
  chopped rosemary

sea salt

freshly ground black pepper

Preheat a hooded barbecue to high. Rub the leg of milk-fed lamb with the olive oil and rosemary and season with salt and pepper. Cover and leave for 10 minutes for the flavours to infuse.

    Seal the leg of lamb on the open grill until golden, then remove and wrap in a double layer of foil. Put the lamb parcel on the flat plate of the barbecue and put the hood down. After 8 minutes, turn the lamb over and cook for a further 8 minutes. Turn the parcel again and cook for another 8 minutes, then remove the lamb from the barbecue and rest for 20 minutes before serving. **Serves 4**

Sophie's Fig and Fennel Bread

While planning the photography sessions for this book, I soon realised I needed help. An SOS went out to Sophie Zalokar, a former apprentice of mine living in Fremantle. A natural cook, she has such a 'feel' for breadmaking that we used to call her the 'bread witch'. I described to her a bread I'd loved in Italy, and the following spectacular result appeared, baked in an old Barossa pudding tin.

750 g dried figs

750 ml verjuice

3½ teaspoons fennel seeds

25 g fresh *or* 2½ teaspoons
   dried yeast

1 teaspoon raw sugar

125 ml warm water

555 g wholemeal plain flour

185 g unbleached strong flour

2 teaspoons extra-virgin
   olive oil

1 teaspoon salt

250 ml thick natural yoghurt

Remove the stems from the figs, then soak the fruit overnight in the verjuice. Next day, strain the figs and retain the verjuice. Purée 1 cup soaked figs in a food processor and roughly chop the remaining fruit.

Dry-roast 2½ teaspoons of the fennel seeds in a frying pan until fragrant, shaking the pan regularly to prevent them from burning. Coarsely grind the roasted seeds in a mortar and pestle and set aside.

Combine the yeast, sugar and warm water in a small bowl and set aside for 5–10 minutes until frothy. In the bowl of an electric mixer fitted with a dough hook, combine the wholemeal and plain flours, olive oil, salt, yoghurt and ground fennel seeds. Add the puréed figs, 100 ml of the reserved verjuice and the yeast mixture. Knead until a soft dough forms.

Turn out the dough – it will be very soft and sticky – onto a floured bench and knead in the chopped figs. Return the dough to the cleaned and lightly oiled bowl. Smear a little oil over the surface of the dough, then cover with plastic film and allow to rise in a draught-free spot until half its volume again (1–1½ hours, depending on weather conditions).

Gently turn the dough out onto a floured bench and divide it into 2 portions (note that you don't knock it back: this is a heavy dough and it will struggle to recover if knocked back the usual way). Put each portion into a bread tin or mould to rise for a further 15 minutes. Meanwhile, preheat the oven to 220°C.

Sprinkle the remaining fennel seeds over the top of each loaf. Bake the loaves for 20 minutes, then reduce the temperature to 180°C and bake for a further 30 minutes. Allow to cool completely on a wire rack before cutting. **Makes 2**

Olive and Rosemary Bread

I find making any bread a truly therapeutic experience, but there is something very special about this one. Here all the ingredients go in together, and the resulting bread has a dark, purplish tinge. If the olives are held back to the second rising, the bread has a totally different finish but is still delicious. For another variation, try toasting the rosemary leaves in a little nut-brown butter first.

15 g fresh *or* 1½ teaspoons
  dried yeast

1 teaspoon castor sugar

300 ml warm water

500 g unbleached strong flour

1 teaspoon salt

2 tablespoons extra-virgin
  olive oil

¼ cup freshly chopped
  rosemary

190 g pitted kalamata olives

Combine the yeast, castor sugar and warm water in a small bowl and set aside for 5–10 minutes until frothy.

In the bowl of an electric mixer fitted with a dough hook, combine the flour, salt, olive oil, rosemary and olives. Gradually add the yeast mixture to make a soft, pliable dough (you may need to add a little more warm water).

Turn the dough out onto a floured bench and knead gently for 5 minutes. Return the dough to the cleaned and lightly oiled bowl and brush it with a little olive oil. Cover the bowl with plastic film and leave to rise in a draught-free spot for about 1 hour or until nearly doubled in volume.

Divide the dough into 2 portions and form into loaves. Brush a baking tray with olive oil and leave the loaves to rise on the oiled tray for a further 20 minutes. Meanwhile, preheat the oven to 220°C.

Bake the loaves for 20 minutes, then reduce the temperature to 180°C and bake for a further 20 minutes. Allow to cool completely on a wire rack before cutting. **Makes 2**

Brioche

The first time I made brioche I followed Jacques Pepin's method in *La Technique* – but it didn't rise, so I presumed I'd failed. I tipped the dough into a plastic rubbish bin and put on the lid. When I put some scraps into the bin the next morning, I found the swollen dough alive and well! I now know that the dough needs to be moist and pliable, and that refrigerating it aids handling.

600 g unbleached strong flour

1 tablespoon dried yeast

1½ tablespoons sugar

1 teaspoon salt

milk

10 free-range eggs

300 g softened unsalted butter

In the bowl of an electric mixer fitted with a dough hook, combine the flour, yeast, sugar and salt. Warm ⅓ cup milk gently in a small saucepan. Whisk 9 of the eggs with the warm milk and add slowly to the flour mixture.

Beat the softened butter into the dough until the dough is soft, shiny and pliable. Cover the bowl with plastic film and leave to rise slowly in the refrigerator overnight.

Turn the dough out onto a floured bench and knead for 10 minutes. Divide it between brioche moulds or bread tins (this amount makes 2 loaves or 1 large, 2 medium or 6 small traditional brioche forms) and leave to rise in a draught-free spot for 40 minutes. Meanwhile, preheat the oven to 200°C.

Whisk the remaining egg and ¼ cup milk and brush over the surface of the dough. Bake for 20 minutes, then reduce the temperature to 180°C and bake for a further 15–20 minutes. Allow to cool completely on a wire rack before cutting.

The Kitchen

The kitchen is the hub of our cottage. It is where we eat all our meals and it is where people always gravitate.

I'd long dreamed of having a large country kitchen, but it wasn't until 1990, after three years of making do in a lean-to fitted with louvres on the back verandah (where it was so cold in winter I often had to cook in a Drizabone), that we started the new one. It is the most significant change we have made to our 1860s stone cottage. The 45 cm thick walls keep the house cool even throughout most heatwaves, so you can imagine the strength of the structure. We took out one such wall to create the kitchen, joining what had been our bedroom and a tiny room with a fireplace so large it could never be lit as the room became suffocatingly hot. As a result, the kitchen now has three sets of double windows and two sets of glass French doors, and is beautifully light.

The room was designed around a marble bench I bought for a song in the late 1970s and which then sat in a shed, waiting for a kitchen. Sadly, I had the timber stripped, as was the fashion then, which meant losing forever the mettwurst-maker's trade name that was emblazoned on it (to this day I can't remember it). The bench is 3 metres long and a metre wide – and the top is one huge, beautiful expanse of marble. Its cool, cool surface is perfect for making pastry and pasta, but in fact I prepare everything on this bench. It runs perpendicular to the stove and oven, with only a metre or so between, creating a contained workspace in what is really a very big kitchen.

The kitchen furniture is made up of old Barossa pieces I've been collecting since I first arrived in the Valley. In the early days I went to clearing sales, where farmers delighted in getting anything for what they considered junk, and later I turned for more special pieces to Kai Liew, of Augusta Antiques

in Adelaide, who has an amazing eye. Kitchen treasures still abound, as the Barossa has such a rich food-related culture. A trip to Pooters (pages 108–9), a haven of the most delicious mix of junk and treasure now located in Tanunda, has always been a highlight for like-minded visitors who love the idea of 'pootering'. While decorative, everything I've collected over the years is also practical – from the old scales that sit alongside my vinegar barrel near the stove to my whimsical, hand-twisted wire strainers and tin pudding or jelly moulds. Treasures line the shelves of my sideboard not as showpieces but as part of our everyday life.

Old cupboards and food safes, still with their original paint, are stacked with preserving jars whose contents sparkle against the old ochre-coloured walls. The paintings that line these walls are all – surprise, surprise – food related and help make the room feel as old as the rest of the house. Even my 1950s double-door stainless steel refrigerator helps maintain an aged tone – it just doesn't seem right having any large, ultramodern appliances here (although our occasional house guests will be pleased to know that it has a new generator and no longer chugs away during the night!).

The windows over the sink look out onto our courtyard and the wood oven. The kitchen benches, made from cured red gum we found on site when we bought the property, by happy coincidence run at the same height as the windowsills. This means that whenever we're barbecuing in the courtyard, rather than carrying all the bits and pieces needed for the meal through the house, we simply swing open the windows and pass everything through. The bench outside the window is also the perfect place for our grandchildren to prop, keeping tabs on everything that's happening inside. This is what our kitchen is all about: it's central to everything we do.

Grape Schiacciata

I thought I could make grape schiacciata until a dinner at our friends the Parronchis in Tuscany. We were celebrating the olive crush of mutual friends, Janet and Stefano, and had enjoyed a tasting of oil from different parts of their grove. I cooked guinea fowl my way, and Stefano brought a huge slab of schiacciata. It was so good, I wrote down all the advice I could glean from him.

20 g fresh *or* 2 teaspoons
  dried yeast
180 ml warm water
castor sugar
150 ml extra-virgin olive oil
2 tablespoons freshly minced
  rosemary
1 kg ripe black grapes
400 g unbleached strong flour
pinch of salt
small sprigs rosemary

Combine the yeast, warm water and 1 teaspoon castor sugar in a small bowl and set aside for 5–10 minutes until frothy. Warm the olive oil in a saucepan and gently 'cook' the minced rosemary for 5 minutes, then set aside to cool. This infuses the oil with a strong rosemary flavour.

Wash the grapes and remove all stems. Put the flour and salt into a bowl, then make a well and add the yeast mixture and half the rosemary-infused oil. Add 400 g of the grapes and mix vigorously, then turn the dough out onto a well-floured bench. Knead the grapes into the dough for 5 minutes – the dough will be very soft and sticky (don't try using a dough hook as it will smash the grapes).

Return the dough to the cleaned and lightly oiled bowl and brush it with a little rosemary oil. Cover the bowl with plastic film and refrigerate the dough overnight or allow it to rise slowly for $1\frac{1}{2}$–2 hours until doubled in volume.

If you have let your dough rise in the refrigerator, allow it to come to room temperature before proceeding (this will take about $1\frac{1}{2}$ hours). Turn out the dough and divide it into 2 portions (there's no need to knock back). Generously brush 2 ovenproof frying pans or 24 cm springform cake tins with the rosemary oil and, using your hands, flatten the dough out over the base of each. Push the remaining grapes into the surface of the dough. Generously brush the dough with the remaining rosemary oil, then sprinkle over the rosemary sprigs and 1 tablespoon castor sugar. Leave to rise in a draught-free spot for about 30 minutes. Meanwhile, preheat the oven to 220°C.

Bake the schiacciate for 20 minutes with a baking tray underneath as the juice from the grapes will bubble up and may overflow. Reduce the temperature to 180°C and bake for a further 10 minutes. Slide out onto a wire rack and serve warm or at room temperature. **Makes 2**

Upside-down Grape Cake

I used to make a grape cake in the Pheasant Farm days and was reminiscing about it with Sophie. In my usual manner, I hadn't written the recipe down, but my memory was that sultana grapes were mixed through the batter and then piled on top. Sophie extended this idea and came up with the following, a totally different but equally moist cake, perfect with preserved fruit and cream for dessert.

80 g sultanas

200 ml verjuice

250 ml red wine

330 g castor sugar

softened unsalted butter

1 large bunch large red grapes

2 free-range eggs

275 g unbleached plain flour

1 teaspoon bicarbonate of
 soda

1 teaspoon cream of tartar

125 ml milk

1 teaspoon pure vanilla extract

Soak the sultanas overnight in the verjuice. Next day, preheat the oven to 200°C. Bring the wine and 240 g of the castor sugar to a boil in a non-reactive saucepan and cook until a thick, slightly caramelised syrup forms. Smear the sides of a 20 cm round cake tin with a little butter before pouring the caramel over the base. Dot the grapes, stems removed, over the caramel and fill in the gaps with the drained verjuice-soaked sultanas.

Cream 100 g butter and the remaining castor sugar until thick and pale, then slowly beat in the eggs. Sift in the flour, bicarbonate of soda and cream of tartar, then mix carefully. Beat in the milk and vanilla extract until the batter is creamy and smooth. Spoon the batter over the grape and caramel base and bake for 30 minutes or until a skewer comes out clean when inserted into the centre of the cake. Leave the cake in the tin for 5 minutes before turning it out onto a plate – the caramel will ooze out, so choose a plate with a lip. Serve warm or at room temperature. **Serves 8**

Plum and Almond Tart

Plums are incredibly underrated and I have a bit of a mission to turn that perception around. I have a variety of plum trees in my orchard that fruit from summer through to early autumn. Like all the fruit in the orchard, the plums are at their best when picked ripe from the tree. What a taste revelation these are! This tart lifts any plum to a new dimension, but especially the best ones.

1 quantity Sour Cream Pastry
  (page 127)
8–10 blood plums

frangipane

130 g almonds
125 g softened unsalted butter
125 g castor sugar
2 free-range eggs, beaten
2 tablespoons unbleached
  plain flour

Make and chill the pastry as instructed. Roll out the chilled pastry until about 3 mm thick and line a loose-bottomed 22 cm flan tin with it. Chill in the freezer for 20 minutes. Meanwhile, preheat the oven to 200°C.

Line the chilled pastry case with foil and then weight it with dried beans or pastry weights and blind bake it for 15 minutes. Remove the foil and beans and return the pastry case to the oven for a further 10 minutes to ensure the pastry is crisp. Set the pastry case aside to cool. Increase the oven temperature to 220°C.

To make the frangipane, roast the almonds on a baking tray for about 5 minutes, shaking the tray to prevent the nuts from burning. Allow to cool, then grind in a food processor or with a mortar and pestle. Cream the butter and sugar until thick and pale, then slowly beat in the eggs. If the butter mixture begins to curdle when adding the eggs, add a little of the flour. Gently mix the nuts and flour into the butter mixture. Reduce the oven temperature to 180°C.

Remove the stones from the plums and cut each plum into 6 pieces. Spoon the prepared frangipane into the pastry case. Arrange the sliced plums in a concentric pattern over the frangipane and bake for 25 minutes. Serve warm. **Serves 8**

frangipane   The almond frangipane used here, the base of the classic Pithiviers (page 168), lends itself to many variations. Try reconstituting dried pears in a light verjuice syrup before adding them to the tart. Fresh or dried apricots are good, too, as are sultanas.

Lemon Poppyseed Cake

We finished off our picnic on pages 96–101 by coming back to the house for a cup of tea and a piece of this cake. It's a wonderfully moist afternoon-tea cake that is just as delicious without the icing. Even better, it keeps for ages and freezes well.

240 g softened unsalted butter

360 g castor sugar

finely grated zest of 4 lemons

75 g poppy seeds

2 teaspoons pure vanilla
  extract

540 g unbleached plain flour

1 tablespoon baking powder

375 ml milk

8 free-range egg whites

lemon icing

2 tablespoons lemon juice

400 g icing sugar

lemon zest (optional)

Preheat the oven to 160°C and grease and line a 24 cm springform cake tin.

Cream the butter and castor sugar until pale and thick. Slowly incorporate the lemon zest, poppy seeds, vanilla extract, flour, baking powder and milk to make a soft batter.

Whisk the egg whites to soft peaks and fold a large spoonful into the batter to loosen it, then fold in the rest. This ensures the whites fold evenly and quickly through the batter without losing too much of the air. Spoon the mixture into the prepared tin and bake for $1\frac{1}{2}$ hours. Turn out onto a wire rack to cool.

To make the icing, warm the lemon juice and icing sugar in a small saucepan and pour over the cooled cake. If desired, finely grate lemon zest over the icing while it is still moist. Allow to set before serving.

Pot-roasted Quinces

This dish was taught to me by Hazel Mader, one of the first female Barons of the Barossa, a title bestowed upon members of the wine community for preserving Valley traditions. Hazel was a consummate hostess (and a soprano of note) and as I was a friend of her daughter Jenny, she happily shared her secret with me, knowing how quinces beguiled me.

6 small Smyrna quinces
1.25 litres water
5 cups sugar
juice of 3 lemons

Rub the down from the quinces and wash the fruit. Pack them tightly into a large, heavy-based non-reactive saucepan, then cover with the water and sugar. Bring the pot to a boil and cook until a jelly starts to form, then reduce the heat to a gentle simmer. Keep the quinces submerged in the syrup by covering them with a piece of foil and weighing them down with an upturned plate. Turn the fruit regularly to ensure even cooking. The quinces will take 5–6 hours of slow cooking to achieve a beautiful ruby glow. Add the lemon juice in the last stages of cooking to cut the sweetness.

Serve the quinces whole with a little of the jelly, and cream or crème anglaise. Serves 6

smyrna quinces   I always choose Smyrna quinces ahead of the more impressive-looking pineapple quince: their flavour is far superior and they withstand the rigours of slow cooking beautifully. (Save pineapple quinces for making jam or when poaching as they break down with long cooking.) If you can, choose quinces with a stem and a leaf attached – they look quite wonderful sitting upright on a serving plate in all their ruby-red, pot-roasted glory.

freezing   The pot-roasted quinces can be frozen, in their jelly, to bring out in the middle of winter.

Quince Yeast Cake

I first tasted a cake like this at the inaugural Australian Symposium of Gastronomy, held in Adelaide in 1984 and the first gathering of foodies I'd ever attended. A loner from the Barossa, I was agog at the line-up of participants, yet delighted to find we were all united by our passion. Jennifer Hillier was responsible for the cake, and I think the basic yeast mixture came from Elizabeth David.

15 g fresh yeast *or*

 1½ teaspoons dried yeast

1 teaspoon castor sugar

warm water

150 g unbleached plain flour

2 small free-range eggs

45 g softened unsalted butter

3 Pot-roasted Quinces

 (see opposite)

reserved jelly from the cooked

 quinces

Mix the yeast and castor sugar with 100 ml warm water in a small bowl and set aside for 5–10 minutes until frothy. Combine the yeast mixture, flour and eggs in the bowl of an electric mixer. Beat in the softened butter until the dough is shiny and soft. If it is dry, add a little extra warm water. Cover the dough with plastic film and leave it in a draught-free spot until doubled in volume, about 2 hours, or leave it overnight in the refrigerator.

If you have let your dough rise in the refrigerator overnight, allow it to come to room temperature before proceeding. Butter a 22 cm springform cake tin and gently flatten the dough over the base of the tin. Cut one of the quinces in half and cut away the core. Arrange both halves in the middle of the dough, cut-side uppermost. Slice the remaining quinces thickly and arrange these around the edge of the dough. Leave the cake to rise in a draught-free spot for 30 minutes.

Meanwhile, preheat the oven to 200°C. Melt a little of the jelly from the quinces and brush this over the surface of the risen cake. Bake for 35–40 minutes. Allow the cake to cool for 10 minutes before removing it from the tin. Serve warm or at room temperature. **Serves 8**

Chocolate and Prune Dessert Cake

This is one of those dishes that started life on a card in the Pheasant Farm Restaurant kitchen that then had notes added and subtracted as the recipe evolved. Now I can't for the life of me remember where the original idea came from. Cooking is all about osmosis – a mental note made about a flavour combination or a technique, a memory of a dish – but I do like to give credit where I can.

350 g pitted prunes

375 ml brandy

240 g unsalted butter

450 g bitter chocolate

1 tablespoon best-quality
   instant coffee granules

8 free-range eggs, separated

115 g unbleached plain flour

120 g castor sugar

ganache

450 g bitter chocolate

⅓ cup best-quality instant
   coffee granules

300 ml cream

Soak the prunes overnight in 125 ml of the brandy.

Next day, preheat the oven to 200°C and line a 28 cm round cake tin or 2 × 20 cm round cake tins with baking paper. Melt the butter in a small saucepan and set it aside to cool a little.

Bring a large saucepan of water to a boil and remove it from the heat. Roughly chop the chocolate and put it with the coffee granules and remaining brandy in a large stainless steel or ceramic bowl. Stand this bowl over the pan of hot water until the chocolate has melted. Stir to combine. Add the egg yolks to the chocolate mixture and then incorporate the melted butter. Sift the flour into the mixture and gently fold it in until combined.

Whisk the egg whites to soft peaks, adding the castor sugar as you go. Fold a little of the whites into the chocolate mixture to lighten it, then pour the chocolate mixture back into the whites, gently folding until evenly combined. Pour the mixture into the prepared cake tin and bake for 20–25 minutes. The cake will rise like a soufflé during baking and will crack on the surface. It will then collapse a little as it cools. Don't fret – this is all meant to happen! Allow the cake to cool in the tin for 45 minutes before turning it out.

Cut the cake in half and gently remove the top layer. Scoop out a little cake from the centre of the bottom layer and blend the crumbs with the drained prunes in a food processor. Fill the cake with the prune mixture and replace the top layer.

Make the ganache by roughly chopping the chocolate and melting it with the coffee and cream in a bowl in a saucepan over a very low heat, stirring to combine once the chocolate has melted. Allow the ganache to cool and set slightly in the refrigerator, then pour it over the cake, smoothing it over the sides until evenly covered. Allow to set completely – you may need to refrigerate the cake to achieve this. Serve with a dollop of double cream. Serves 12

port and sherry   Instead of using brandy to soak the prunes, try port or flor fino sherry instead.

figs and cherries   I've also made this cake with ripe figs or poached sour cherries, but the combination of prunes and chocolate is probably the most heavenly of all.

Fig Galette

There are so many ways to cook with really ripe figs – and this is one of them. A galette is a rustic style of sweet or savoury open pie, so don't be tempted whatever you do to fuss over its appearance. It will be more true to type if simply put together with seasonal fruits and jams, layers of finely sliced potato and rosemary, or a mixture of soft cheeses.

180 g fig jam

8 large ripe black figs

rough puff pastry

450 g unbleached plain flour

450 g chilled unsalted butter

½ teaspoon salt

250 ml cold water

To make the pastry, tip the flour onto a bench and make a well in the centre. Dice the butter and put it and the salt into the well, then, using a pastry scraper, cut the butter into the flour. Make a well again and pour in 180 ml of the cold water. Using the pastry scraper, work the flour and butter into the water, adding the remaining water if necessary, to make a firm but pliable dough. Gather the pastry into a ball, then cut this in half and gently pat each piece into a disc and wrap it in plastic film. Refrigerate one piece of pastry for 20 minutes, and date the other and put it into the freezer for next time you're making a galette or need rough puff.

Roll the pastry out to make a rectangle about 1.5 cm thick. Keeping the longer side of the rectangle parallel to the bench, fold both ends into the centre – it will look like an open book. Then fold one side over the other to 'close the book'. Cover and refrigerate the pastry again for 20 minutes. Repeat this step twice.

Preheat the oven to 200°C. Roll out the pastry to make a round 30–35 cm in diameter and about 5 mm thick. Spread a thick layer of fig jam over the pastry. Thickly slice the figs and arrange these on the pastry in overlapping concentric circles, leaving a 5 cm border. Gently fold the pastry border over the figs. Bake the galette for 25–30 minutes until the pastry is golden brown and the figs are just cooked. **Serves 8**

rough puff pastry   Don't be afraid of giving this a go – it's perfect for those who are always in a hurry or are unsure of themselves in the kitchen. While it's not true puff pastry, it's only a few turns short of the real thing and a mile better than any commercial product. It freezes well, too, so it's worth making a full quantity rather than just the amount needed in this recipe. Wrap it well and it will be fine frozen for up to 3 months.

Pears with Red-wine Butter and Almond-and-buttermilk Blancmange

The sole remainder of our three 150-year-old pear trees is so tall it might be mistaken for an oak. While the spring blossom is breath-taking, the fruit is not, but I've planted new trees to keep the tradition alive as pears thrive in the Barossa. I give the pear-and-red-wine combination a new twist here, and love the way the blancmange wobbles as it is presented at the table.

6 ripe pears

red-wine butter

240 g castor sugar

500 ml red wine

250 g softened unsalted butter

almond-and-buttermilk blancmange

250 g almonds

200 ml buttermilk

200 ml water

80 g sugar

4 gelatine leaves

350 ml cream

To make the red-wine butter, boil the sugar and wine in a non-reactive saucepan until thick and syrupy. Allow to cool slightly. Blend the red-wine syrup and butter in a food processor, then chill.

To make the blancmange, preheat the oven to 220°C. Roast the almonds on a baking tray for about 5 minutes, shaking the tray to prevent the nuts from burning. Allow to cool, then grind in a food processor or with a mortar and pestle. Soak the ground almonds in the buttermilk and water for 1 hour. Squeeze the liquid out through a muslin cloth and discard the almonds. Gently warm the resulting almond milk and add the sugar, stirring to dissolve it.

Soften the gelatine leaves in a little cold water, then drain and squeeze out the excess water. Stir the softened leaves into the warm almond milk until dissolved, then chill.

Whip the cream until soft peaks form, then fold this into the chilled almond milk and pour into 6 dariole moulds (I sometimes just use pretty glasses). Allow to set in the refrigerator for 2 hours.

Preheat the oven to 220°C. Cut the pears in half (leaving the skins on) and scoop out the core with a melon baller. Lie the pears in a deep baking dish and cover with chunks of the chilled red-wine butter. Roast for 20 minutes, turning the pears over halfway through the cooking. If the pears need more caramelising, stand them under the griller just before serving.

Serve the warm pear halves with a blancmange alongside. If you want, you can turn out the blancmanges: just dip the base of the mould into hot water and invert each blancmange onto a waiting plate. **Serves 6**

Star-anise Ice-cream

Back in the days of the Pheasant Farm Restaurant, we churned the ice-cream as the first guests arrived, and gave leftovers to staff to take home as the flavour diminishes very quickly. Making ice-cream is simple if you have the right appliance – just make sure the bowl of your machine has been well frozen beforehand. And remember: the final flavour will only be as good as the quality of the base ingredients.

600 ml milk

400 ml cream

4 star anise

10 free-range egg yolks

60 g castor sugar

Bring the milk and cream to a boil with the star anise. Whisk the egg yolks with the castor sugar in a large bowl, then whisk in the hot milk mixture. Return the mixture to the saucepan (or stand the bowl over a pan of simmering water) and cook very gently, stirring constantly, until the custard is thick enough to coat the back of a spoon. Allow to cool, stirring occasionally, then chill before churning in an ice-cream machine according to the manufacturer's instructions. **Makes 1 litre**

making ice-cream   Homemade ice-cream starts with a custard base, which puts some people off immediately. But if you follow a few basic principles, custards are a dream to make and nothing like anything you can buy (the same goes for the ice-cream). If you haven't made a custard before, stand a bowl over a saucepan of simmering water rather than attempting to cook the custard in the saucepan over direct heat. It is important that the custard cooks slowly and gently as it curdles easily. There is no way to retrieve a fully curdled custard: unless you manage to see those first signs of graininess and quickly add some chilled cream or milk to inhibit the cooking, you will need to start again. Remember to keep stirring and to avoid letting the custard become too hot and you'll be fine.

Sherri's Rotegrütze

This simple dessert epitomises Barossan culture, where the local influences the traditional. Silesian migrants brought the recipe when they settled in the Valley in the 1840s. In their homeland they had made it with berries; using what was to hand in the Barossa they made it with grapes, often mataro or shiraz. Today, rotegrütze makes regular public appearances, especially during the Vintage Festival.

very ripe black grapes
(preferably shiraz)

sago

To extract the juice from the grapes, either use the finest setting on a food mill or purée the grapes in a food processor and strain the juice through a sieve, pushing down on the solids to extract as much juice as possible. If a large amount of juice is required, gently heat whole bunches of grapes in a large pot until the grapes are soft enough that the stems can be pulled away from the berries easily. This mixture can then be strained and the skins and seeds discarded. The resulting juice has a slightly thickened consistency compared to the juice retrieved using a food mill.

Measure the juice into a non-reactive saucepan and bring it gently to a simmer. For every 550 ml juice, gradually stir in 2 tablespoons sago. Simmer gently, stirring occasionally, until the sago is clear. This will take 45–50 minutes.

Pour the rotegrütze into a serving dish and allow it to cool, then chill and allow to set slightly. Serve with rich, runny cream.

Pithiviers

While this is a classic French dessert, I offer it here with rough puff rather than the fully turned puff pastry, so it has quite a different finish from the traditional version. I have friends who so love making pithiviers, down to the puff, that we have had dinners with up to three versions on the table so that we could taste one against the other!

1 quantity Rough Puff Pastry
 (page 162)
1 free-range egg
1 tablespoon milk

filling

125 g almonds
60 g softened unsalted butter
100 g castor sugar
1 × 61 g free-range egg
1 free-range egg yolk
1/3 cup self-raising flour
1/2 teaspoon pure vanilla
 extract
2 tablespoons brandy
2 tablespoons cream

Make and chill the pastry as instructed.

To make the filling, preheat the oven to 220°C. Roast the almonds on a baking tray for about 5 minutes, shaking the tray to prevent the nuts from burning. Allow to cool a little, then grind finely in a food processor. Cream the butter and castor sugar in an electric mixer until pale and thick. Add the whole egg and egg yolk and beat for another minute, then add the ground almonds and the remaining ingredients and mix until well combined. Refrigerate until chilled.

Roll the chilled pastry out into two rounds, making one slightly thinner and larger than the other. Put the thicker sheet of pastry on a large greased baking tray. Whisk the egg and milk together and brush this lightly over the pastry. Mound the chilled filling in the centre of the pastry, allowing a 3 cm border and making the middle its highest point. Position the other pastry sheet on top and gently press down evenly to remove any air pockets. Cut a scalloped border around the edge of the filling, making sure there is at least 1 cm between the filling and where the cut comes in. This will stop any leakages – note, too, that if there is too much filling, the top layer of pastry will split during baking. Refrigerate the pithiviers for 20 minutes.

Meanwhile, preheat the oven to 220°C. Lightly brush the pastry with the egg wash and score the scalloped border in a cross-hatched pattern. Score a concentric pattern from the middle of the mound to the base. Bake for 10 minutes, then reduce the temperature to 180°C and bake for a further 25–35 minutes until golden brown. Serve warm with double cream. Serves 8

Sauternes and Grape Jelly

I have collected kitchen paraphernalia, all useful, for years, frequenting Pooters (see page 149) and Pioneer Antiques of Tanunda for jelly moulds, tins, old linen and crockery and so on. Having said that, while I love using an old-fashioned mould to set this jelly (see below opposite), don't discount just using nicely shaped cups – once turned out, the jelly will still be imposing.

6 gelatine leaves

cold water

475 ml Sauternes *or* other
  dessert wine

1 kg sultana grapes

To make the jelly, soften the gelatine leaves in a little cold water, then drain and squeeze out the excess water. Bring the wine to a simmer in a non-reactive saucepan, then turn off the heat and stir in the softened gelatine until dissolved. Allow to cool.

Pour a little of the cooled jelly mixture into the base of your chosen mould or moulds (a large mould should hold at least 1 litre) and allow it to just set. Arrange a layer of grapes, stems removed, on top, then add a little more jelly to just cover the grapes. Allow to set in the refrigerator. Continue to build up the layers of grapes by allowing them to set in the jelly before adding more. This will ensure the grapes are evenly dispersed through the jelly. (If the remaining jelly starts to become too firm before you need it, simply warm it a little and then allow it to cool before adding the next layer of jelly and grapes.)

Turn the jelly or jellies out of the mould by running the base quickly under a hot tap and then inverting the jelly onto a serving plate. Serve with Lemon Biscuits (see opposite). Serves 8

Lemon Biscuits

I like to serve these delicate, lemony biscuits alongside Sauternes and Grape Jelly (see opposite), but they're equally delicious with a short black at the end of a meal.

125 g softened unsalted butter

200 g icing sugar

200 g unbleached plain flour

finely grated zest of 2 small
  lemons

½ teaspoon pure vanilla
  extract

5 free-range egg whites

Preheat the oven to 220°C and grease and line baking trays with baking paper. Cream the butter and icing sugar in an electric mixer until pale and thick, then add the flour, lemon zest and vanilla extract. Whisk the egg whites to soft peaks and fold gently into the butter mixture.

Pipe 5 cm lengths of the mixture onto the baking trays and bake for 8–10 minutes. Transfer the biscuits to a wire rack to cool. **Makes 25–30**

summerautumnwinterspring

A Kitchen Supper Sometime during winter the program for the Barossa Music Festival is launched. The festival itself isn't held until the first week of October, which always seems eons away, but the flurry of putting the program to bed and letting everyone know about the forthcoming event always sees the months disappear in a flash.

This is a time for the locals – the festival would not be the internationally acclaimed event it is today if not for the continued support of the inhabitants of the Valley. Over the years, John Russell has gathered the local community together for the launch – drinks and nibbles are served, a speech about the program is given, and all present enjoy a preview of one of the acts that's to appear at the festival proper, then everyone disbands to have supper somewhere. Not that we ever need to be urged to get involved: music is incredibly important in the life of the Valley, and Barossans love a party!

I have to say my favourite launch of all during the years I've been involved was

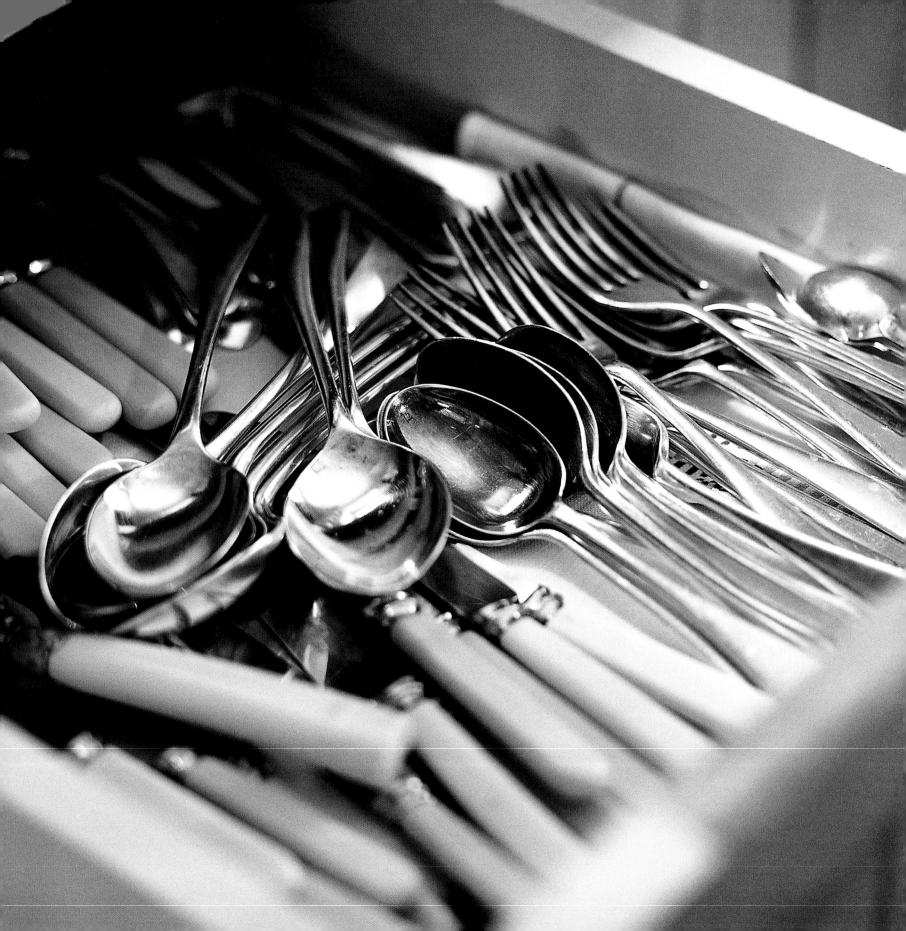

one at Yalumba. We never know how many are likely to turn up to these nights, so decided to serve something easy: flatbread with simple toppings (page 67). On the night, the Cask Hall was thick with people and the wineries, as ever, had donated plenty of wine. But what a crowd, and how hungry they were! A team of us kept pace by making more and more yeast bases, topping them with anything we could find in the fridges. My everlasting memory will be of the head of our committee, the lovely Mary Downer – Lady Downer to others – pushing her way through the crowd to serve tray after tray of the piping-hot bread.

I love serving supper after such an event – I've found success is assured if you start with happy friends already energised by music and a glass or two of wine. One dish only is my motto, with perhaps cheese to follow. I love the feeling of largesse and simplicity, and enjoy having my friends around as I cook, so preparing risotto on such occasions makes perfect sense.

I use a huge paella pan when making risotto for a crowd, as I did when preparing cuttlefish risotto (page 198) last year. The pan requires a large cooking surface, but luckily one side of my stove is a simmer pad that can be turned up high in the centre when a whoosh of heat is needed.

With the stock for the risotto made during the afternoon, all I did before the performance was fold the serviettes, fill a favourite green vase with low-flying blooms, pull out spoons and forks, and make sure the salt pot and pepper grinder were full and the bottle of extra-virgin olive oil was to hand.

Our very old, metre-wide kitchen table has stretchers on each end, but no way can it seat twelve, so I got several guests to bring in an old favourite, a square table whose legs still bear the original steely-blue paint. (I use this table for many things: it travels from room to room either to have books stacked on it, to show off a huge vase of flowers or for extending the table on occasions like this.) With the table in place and the serviettes and cutlery distributed, everyone was soon standing around, glass in hand, talking loudly over my music selection – which changed from Maria Callas to Joe Cocker at one stage, I noticed. Jane, who had never been in the kitchen before, wandered from piece to piece of kitchen paraphernalia and treasured memorabilia, absorbed in that delightful way of someone understanding you more because of the things with which you surround yourself.

There was a heated moment when Colin thought I should turn the music down, but I wanted to hold off until the risotto was cooked. It's definitely a dish you can make with some flamboyance and your mind on your guests as well as the food! Because the huge pan had rather taken over the stove, I had to pull out my electric frying pan to deal with the kilos of cuttlefish. It worked brilliantly, although I could only cook a cupful at a time and had to call for help from onlookers when the risotto needed attention. Adding the cuttlefish ink to the rice drew lots of comments and when the stock became inky and thick, I knew all was nearly ready. Then it was in with the pan-fried cuttlefish, lots of parsley and a swirl of extra-virgin olive oil.

The paella pan proved too large for the table, so I put it on a wooden slab on my marble bench and everyone helped themselves. This made it all the more fun – it was so casual, everyone was involved in a haphazard way and the kitchen kept everyone connected. The ideal supper.

Flo Beer's Pickled Quince

My dear, late mum-in-law, Flo, gave me this recipe the first time I met the family in 1969 at their Mallala home north of Adelaide. Our cooking worlds were so very different, yet that meal – pickled pork with pickled quince (page 225) – has become entrenched in our own family's traditions. I love pickled quince for its unique flavour, and, of course, the memories of a wonderful mother-in-law.

quinces

lemon juice

white-wine vinegar

sugar

cloves

peppercorns

cayenne pepper (optional)

Peel and quarter the quinces, then, to prevent discoloration, immediately steep them in a sink of water to which lemon juice has been added.

Transfer the quince to a non-reactive preserving pan and almost cover with vinegar. To each 600 ml vinegar used, add 2 cups sugar, 1 teaspoon cloves and 1 teaspoon peppercorns. Add a little cayenne pepper to taste, if desired.

Boil the quince until it is soft and light pink, about 25 minutes. Allow to cool, then transfer to sterilised jars and spoon in the pickling solution. Seal, then invert the jars to create a vacuum. Leave for several weeks before opening.

Fennel Soup with Fresh Oysters

We are partners in Charlick's, a wine bar and bistro in Adelaide. One night James, a young chef who served his apprenticeship in Damien Pignolet's Sydney kitchens, made this sublime soup for me. It is fresh and delicate, yet can be a meal on its own if you're generous with the oysters. For another twist, you could add cream towards the end, or saffron to the braising fennel.

2 large fennel bulbs

8 shallots

8 cloves garlic

¼ cup olive oil

430 ml jellied good-quality
  fish stock

sea salt

freshly ground black pepper

24 freshly shucked oysters

½ cup washed chervil leaves

Remove the fronds and cores from the fennel bulbs, then roughly chop the bulbs. You need 1 kg chopped fennel to proceed. Roughly chop the shallots and garlic, then gently sauté these in the olive oil in a large non-reactive pot until translucent. Add the chopped fennel and toss to coat with the oil. Add the fish stock and bring the pot to a simmer. Cook slowly for 20 minutes until the fennel has just softened but still retains its soft-green colour.

Purée the stock and vegetables in a food processor or blender, then pass the soup through a fine sieve to remove as much fibre as possible. Season with salt and pepper. Ladle into warm soup bowls, or transfer to a tureen, and float the oysters on the top, as shown opposite. Sprinkle the chervil over the surface and serve immediately. Serves 8

Minestrone with Cavolo Nero

While Stephanie Alexander made a wonderful minestrone when we were in Tuscany some years ago, it was just a little early for cavolo nero, a traditional addition. This long-leafed cabbage (see opposite) retains its texture during cooking, turns almost black, and has a unique flavour. I now grow it in my garden, and add it to my own version of minestrone, modelled on that of Stephanie's.

275 g dried lima beans

3 onions

3 cloves garlic

2 carrots

2 sticks celery

olive oil

20 g butter

6 large sprigs thyme

3 rashers bacon

rind from a piece of

   Parmigiano-Reggiano

2 small fresh bay leaves

1 × 410 g can peeled and

   chopped Roma tomatoes

2.5 litres chicken stock

8–10 large cavolo nero leaves

2 zucchini

100 g green beans

sea salt

freshly ground black pepper

good-quality extra-virgin

   olive oil

Soak the lima beans overnight in double their volume of water. Next day, roughly chop the onions and garlic and dice the carrots and celery. Heat 125 ml olive oil and the butter in a stockpot until the butter is nut-brown, then gently sauté the onion and garlic until translucent. Tie the thyme together with kitchen string and add it to the pot with the drained lima beans, carrot, celery, bacon, cheese rind and bay leaves and toss to coat with the olive oil and butter.

Add the chopped tomato and 2 litres of the chicken stock, then stir and bring to a boil. Turn down to a gentle simmer and allow to cook slowly for 1½ hours. You may need to add a little more stock during cooking, so keep an eye on the pot.

Remove the stems from the cavolo nero and shred the leaves, then toss these in a little olive oil over heat and add them to the pot and simmer for another 10 minutes. Shortly before serving, dice the zucchini and slice the beans and cook these in the soup until just tender. Season with salt and pepper. To serve, remove the bacon, cheese rind and bundle of thyme, then ladle the minestrone into warm, wide soup bowls and drizzle over a little extra-virgin olive oil. **Serves 8**

Artichokes in Verjuice

We grow masses of artichokes in our garden – take my word for it, the artichoke picked and cooked immediately is the sweetest imaginable. One night, without a lemon in the house, I used verjuice to inhibit discoloration and found it not only worked but was a great flavour combination. These artichokes can be added to an antipasto platter or bean dish or served as an accompaniment.

verjuice

artichokes

extra-virgin olive oil

Pour a good quantity of verjuice into a large, non-reactive bowl. Prepare the artichokes by stripping away all the petals to reveal the choke and heart. Using a teaspoon, scoop out the choke and trim the stem with a paring knife. Put the prepared artichokes into the verjuice immediately to prevent discoloration.

Remove the artichokes from the verjuice and blot each one dry. Pour olive oil into a frying pan to a depth of 2 cm and heat. Shallow-fry the artichokes, turning them frequently, until crisp and golden on the outside and meltingly tender on the inside. Take care that the oil does not become too hot during this process. Transfer the artichokes to kitchen paper to drain and cool a little.

varieties   Artichokes with thick green petals, rather than thinner purple ones, are more appropriate here as the choke is smaller and the heart larger.

Broadbean Salad

Broad beans are, unusually, a childhood favourite of mine, and the speciality of an eccentric aunt who was a wonderful gardener but who cooked whatever beans made the pot after our podding until they were a muddy green – and still I loved them. Aunty Glad would never have peeled them in a fit, but I have for this salad, the colours, flavours and textures of which combine beautifully.

2 kg young broad beans

unsalted butter

sea salt

extra-virgin olive oil

3 thick slices good country-
   style bread

1 clove garlic

50 g mature goat's cheese

100 g prosciutto

flat-leaf parsley

1 generous handful
   lamb's lettuce

lemon vinaigrette

1/3 cup extra-virgin olive oil

1 tablespoon lemon juice

sea salt

freshly ground black pepper

Shell the broad beans and simmer them with a knob of butter and a good pinch of sea salt in just enough water to cover until tender, then drain. Drizzle the beans with olive oil and spread them out on a baking tray to cool. Once the beans are cool enough to handle, peel and discard the outer skins – I don't do this for every broadbean dish but it's worth the effort for this salad as the brilliant-green beans look amazing, as you can see in the picture below.

Lightly grill the bread and rub one side with the cut clove of garlic, then tear the bread into rough pieces and put them into a serving bowl. Crumble the goat's cheese, then cut the prosciutto into strips and pick the parsley leaves away from the stems, then mix all these with the bread, broad beans and lamb's lettuce. Make the vinaigrette by combining all the ingredients, then drizzle over the salad and toss gently to combine. Serve immediately. Serves 4–6

Cardoons in Verjuice and Extra-virgin Olive Oil

Cardoons, prized for their stalks, have an intense flavour very similar to an artichoke. I only use stalks that are protected from the sun. A friend from Italy told me that in his garden he alternates a row of cardoons with a row of corn, as his family has always done. The corn supports the growing cardoons until it is harvested, when the tall cardoons bend over and pile up, thus protecting the stems.

water

verjuice

6 inner cardoon stalks

125 ml extra-virgin olive oil

freshly chopped flat-leaf
  parsley

sea salt

freshly ground black pepper

Fill a bowl with water and pour in a good splash of verjuice (you can also use lemon juice or vinegar). String the cardoon stalks with a potato peeler, then transfer to the acidulated water to prevent discoloration.

Simmer the cardoons in 125 ml verjuice in a non-reactive frying pan until tender, about 10 minutes. Remove the pan from the heat and add the olive oil, then add parsley and salt and pepper to taste. Serve warm with lamb, pork or offal (they're delicious with the liver brochettes on page 211). Serves 2

older stalks   Traditionally, older cardoon stalks are cooked in a blanc in a non-reactive pot after they have been trimmed and steeped in acidulated water, as mentioned above. Make a slurry of 1 tablespoon flour and a little water, then stir this into a pot of water with 1 teaspoon lemon juice and 1 tablespoon olive oil. Bring the water to a boil, but make sure it doesn't boil over. Boil the cardoons in the blanc until tender, about 30 minutes, before proceeding with the above recipe. The older stalks also make great fritters: purée the boiled stalks, then add an egg and some flour and deep-fry the mixture in spoonfuls.

in the oven   When we were doing the photography for this book, we cooked the cardoons in the oil in which we had shallow-fried artichokes (page 186), then finished them off in our wood-fired oven. The result was rich and full of flavour – a wonderful accompaniment to saltbush mutton (page 222). To do this in your own wood-fired or domestic oven, prepare the stalks as above and blanch any older, thick stalks in boiling water until just tender enough that the tip of small sharp knife slides through easily. Young cardoon stalks don't need this treatment. Gently shallow-fry the cardoons in olive oil, and then transfer them to the oven to continue cooking slowly. The cardoons may take up to 45 minutes in a domestic oven set at 200°C. They took 25 minutes in my wood oven, which was very hot at the time. The difference in flavour is that all food cooked in a wood oven benefits from the intense heat that ensures fast and even caramelisation. The ingredients maintain their texture and their flavour is heightened.

Salad Greens with Ruby Grapefruit, Walnuts and Walnut Oil Dressing

This salad, pictured opposite, is great served with pan-fried brains or something similarly rich. Ruby grapefruit, with a blush like pink Champagne, is less acidic than the usual variety and provides a zing that lifts this salad beyond the ordinary. If you like, drizzle the roasted walnuts with a little walnut oil and toss them over heat before adding them to the salad.

55 g walnuts

2 large handfuls salad greens
  (lamb's lettuce, rocket, salad
  burnet, sorrel, cress)

2 ruby grapefruit

walnut oil dressing

25 ml verjuice

100 ml walnut oil

squeeze of lemon juice

sea salt

freshly ground black pepper

Preheat the oven to 220°C. Roast the walnuts on a baking tray for about 5 minutes, shaking the tray to prevent the nuts from burning. If they are not fresh season's, rub the walnuts in a clean tea towel to remove the bitter skins. Allow to cool.

Wash, dry and pick through the greens thoroughly. Peel the grapefruit, then cut the segments away with a sharp paring knife to leave all pith and membrane behind. Make the dressing by whisking the verjuice into the walnut oil with the lemon juice, then season it with salt and pepper. Toss the greens with the grapefruit segments and roasted walnuts, then dress and serve the salad immediately. Serves 4

Fennel, Lemon and Olive Salad

The aniseedy flavour of fennel and the piquant yet slightly sweet note of Meyer lemon make this salad so fresh. Choose a fruity, almost green extra-virgin oil, and pluck the leaves from the parsley that's surviving the winter rather than chop them.

2 round fennel bulbs

2 Meyer lemons

freshly plucked flat-leaf
  parsley leaves

fruity extra-virgin olive oil

sea salt

freshly ground black pepper

¼ cup tiny black olives

Cut the fennel bulbs in half lengthwise, then slice them very thinly. Slice 1½ lemons very thinly, too, then juice the remaining half. Toss the fennel and lemon slices with the lemon juice and some parsley, then add olive oil, salt and pepper to taste and finally mix through the olives. Serves 4

tiny olives   I like to use the wild olives found throughout the Barossa for their intense flavour; otherwise look for tiny niçoise or kalamata. The key here is that the olives are small.

Smoked Bantam Eggs with Sorrel Rémoulade

I've always wanted to smoke eggs and crackle the shells so that they craze like Chinese 'thousand-year' eggs, and now that I have my own portable smoker, shown below with olives alongside the eggs, I can. Bantam eggs made this dish very special because the yolks are particularly creamy. The sorrel rémoulade helps cut the richness of the eggs, photographed below right on a friend's amusing plate.

8 bantam eggs

salt

freshly ground black pepper

sorrel rémoulade

2 generous handfuls sorrel

extra-virgin olive oil

2 hardboiled free-range
  egg yolks

½ teaspoon red-wine vinegar

1 free-range egg yolk

1 teaspoon Dijon mustard

sea salt

freshly ground black pepper

3 cornichons

1 tablespoon tiny capers

To make the rémoulade, remove the stems from the sorrel and shred the leaves (you need 1 cup tightly packed shredded sorrel). Heat a little olive oil in a frying pan, then sauté the sorrel until wilted. Put the sorrel into a sieve and press out as much liquid as possible. Leave to cool.

Pound the hardboiled egg yolks to a paste with a drop of the vinegar in a mortar and pestle (or carefully in a food processor), then stir in the egg yolk and mustard and season with salt and pepper. Pour 150 ml olive oil into the egg mixture in a slow, thin stream, incorporating it into the mixture as you go (this is the same technique used when making mayonnaise). Once all the oil has been incorporated and the sauce is thick, finely chop the cornichons and fold these into the sauce with the capers and wilted sorrel. Season with salt and pepper, and if needed, a squeeze of lemon. The rémoulade should be piquant.

Prepare your smoker. Meanwhile, soft-boil the bantam eggs in salted water. Gently and evenly crack the shells by tapping them lightly on a hard surface, but do not peel them. Put the eggs into the smoker, then cover and smoke for 10 minutes.

Peel and slice the eggs, then arrange on a serving dish. Spoon on small dollops of the rémoulade and season with pepper. Serves 4

Artichoke Omelette

How do I cope with a glut of artichokes? I eat them for breakfast, lunch and dinner (but not on the same day!) Artichokes have an affinity with eggs and are especially good in a frittata or omelette. If you're cooking more than one omelette, however, prepare and cook the artichokes in advance.

unsalted butter

extra-virgin olive oil

1 Artichoke in Verjuice
  (page 186)

verjuice *or* lemon juice

3 free-range eggs

20 g gruyère *or* raclette

sea salt

freshly ground black pepper

freshly chopped flat-leaf
  parsley

Cook a knob of butter until nut-brown in a heavy-based non-reactive frying pan (I keep a pan exclusively for making omelettes – the base remains scratch-free, so my omelettes never stick.) Add a spoonful of olive oil to inhibit burning.

Slice the artichoke thinly and drizzle immediately with verjuice or lemon juice to prevent discoloration. Toss the artichoke in the butter until cooked through, then set aside and keep warm.

Whisk the eggs lightly in a bowl, then dice the cheese and add to the eggs with salt and pepper. Stand the frying pan over heat, then add a knob of butter. Allow the butter to sizzle, making sure it coats the sides of the pan as well as the base, then draw off any excess butter. Tip the egg mixture into the pan and allow it to cook for 6 seconds.

Here I borrow Jacques Pepin's words from *La Technique* – this book taught me how to make perfect omelettes many years ago. 'With the flat side of a fork in one hand, stir the eggs in a circular motion. Simultaneously, with the other hand, shake the pan back and forth in a continuous movement so that the eggs coagulate uniformly. Lift up the pan slightly while the eggs are cooking so that the "scrambled" eggs end up piled up toward the front of the pan. Run your fork along the side of the pan under the front of the omelette.' This is the trick to making sure the middle of the omelette is moist and that you don't end up with an evenly cooked 'roll' of egg.

Put the still-warm artichoke down the middle of the omelette and sprinkle on a little parsley. Lift the side of the omelette closest to you and fold it over the middle. Give the handle of the pan a little tap, with the pan at a slight angle, so that the opposite side folds back over the folded omelette. Turn out onto a warm plate and eat immediately. Makes 1

preserved artichokes   Don't try substituting preserved artichokes in this recipe – the vinegar makes them too strong. Barbecued artichokes from a deli may be suitable, but only if they're not in a vinegary dressing.

Bantam Egg Salad

Not everyone has a friend on the next farm who keeps bantams – I'm very lucky! I hesitate giving a cooking time for these eggs as everything depends on their size – the key to perfection here is having them still almost runny – but I was surprised to find that mine only took a minute less than my usual eggs. A delicious lunch for when the weather starts to improve.

2 handfuls salad greens
  (rocket, cress, salad burnet)
4 boiled waxy potatoes
8 softboiled and peeled
  bantam eggs
8 Artichokes in Verjuice
  (page 186)
4 anchovy fillets
½ cup tiny wild olives
sea salt
freshly ground black pepper
extra-virgin olive oil

Wash and dry the salad greens thoroughly, then arrange a bed of greens on each plate. Cut the potatoes into quarters and divide between the plates with the bantam eggs and artichokes. Drape the anchovy fillets over the eggs and scatter over the wild olives. Season with salt and pepper and drizzle over a little olive oil. **Serves 4**

quail eggs   If the diminutive size of bantam eggs appeals, as it does to me, but you can't find them, you can also use quail eggs here. Just watch the cooking time.

Penne with Rapini, Almonds and Currants

I am never without good dried pasta and am spoilt as we import small quantities from an artisanal producer in Greve, Chianti, for our Farm Shop. What a difference great flour and slow drying make to pasta. Rapini, a bitter member of the Brassica family, is seldom seen for sale but easy to grow, and marries well with the bittersweet Sicilian flavours used here. Top-quality extra-virgin olive oil only, please.

⅓ cup currants
⅓ cup verjuice
4 large handfuls rapini
3 onions
6 cloves garlic
500 g good-quality penne
extra-virgin olive oil
⅓ cup toasted almond flakes
sea salt
freshly ground black pepper
160 g freshly shaved
　Parmigiano-Reggiano

Put the currants and verjuice in a bowl and soak overnight, or microwave them on high for 30 seconds.

When you are ready to eat, remove the leaves from the rapini and discard the coarser stalks. Cut the remaining stalks into 5 cm lengths and roughly chop the greens and any flowers. Roughly chop the onions and garlic.

Bring a large pot of salted water to a boil and cook the penne with 1 tablespoon olive oil according to the manufacturer's instructions. Meanwhile, heat 2 tablespoons olive oil in a large frying pan and gently sauté the onion and garlic until translucent. Add the rapini and toss it over heat until it is just tender but still retains a little crunch. Fold through the drained currants and the toasted almond flakes.

Divide the pasta between 4 warm plates, or tip it into a large bowl, and pile the rapini mixture on top. Sprinkle with salt and pepper and drizzle with a little more olive oil. Serve with freshly shaved Parmigiano-Reggiano. **Serves 4**

Cuttlefish Risotto

When I served this at our kitchen supper (pages 176–81) everyone oohed and aahed as the rice turned grey and then jet-black after the ink was added. Cuttlefish ink is superior to squid but less available, while octopus ink is more plentiful but less sweet. Any ink can be frozen for later use, and sachets of squid ink sold at good food stores simplify things even further.

1 kg cuttlefish *or* squid
(ink sacs intact)

1 lemon

3 cloves garlic

extra-virgin olive oil

sea salt

freshly ground black pepper

1.5–2 litres fish stock

100 g unsalted butter

1 onion

400 g arborio rice

125 ml verjuice *or*
dry white wine

3 sachets squid ink (optional)

½ cup freshly chopped
flat-leaf parsley

Remove the ink sacs from the cuttlefish and set them aside: the silvery sac is quite hard and located between the eyes – be careful that you don't pierce it. (You need 2 cuttlefish ink sacs for this dish, or 3 sachets of squid ink – see comment opposite.) Cut the tentacles away from the head and set aside. Slip the bone from the middle of each cuttlefish and discard (or give them to your aviary birds or chooks), then clean out each tube using a long-handled spoon and discard the guts. Strip away the tough purplish-black outer membrane. Run the tubes under cold water and pat them dry with kitchen paper. Cut the tentacles into small pieces and the tubes into strips.

Remove the zest of the lemon in one long strip, then juice the lemon. Finely chop the garlic and gently sauté it in a little olive oil in a large, heavy-based frying pan until it begins to colour. Turn up the heat and add half the cuttlefish and season. As soon as the cuttlefish turns white, remove it from the pan. Sauté the remaining cuttlefish, adding a little more oil if necessary. Deglaze the pan with half the lemon juice, then check the seasoning and add the lemon zest. Toss all the cuttlefish together, then set aside in a bowl.

Heat the stock in a saucepan and keep at a gentle simmer. Finely chop the onion. Melt the butter in the cleaned frying pan and add a splash of olive oil to inhibit burning, then gently sauté the onion until translucent. Turn up the heat and add the rice, stirring well until it is gleaming.

Pour in the verjuice and stir until it has evaporated. Add the first ladleful of stock, stirring to incorporate it, then turn down the heat to moderate. Continue cooking, adding a ladleful of stock as the last is absorbed and stirring all the while. The texture of the risotto is a personal choice, which is why I suggest 1.5–2 litres stock. The rice will take about 20 minutes to cook and shouldn't go beyond being al dente.

If the ink is at all grainy, pound the ink sacs in a mortar and pestle. Squeeze the ink from the 2 sacs or 3 sachets into the risotto, then stir in all the cuttlefish. Check for seasoning – you may need the balance of the lemon juice – and stir the parsley through the risotto. Serve immediately *without* the usual Parmigiano-Reggiano. **Serves 4**

ink sachets   Be warned: this product comes in varying forms depending on the brand. The most common is a single envelope of ink. However, I have also seen very large sachets, each divided into 4 envelopes. Each of these 4 envelopes is the equivalent of 1 of the more usual variety. I used 3 of the very large sachets when making the risotto for the kitchen supper for 12 people descibed on pages 176–81, so, if cooking for 4 people, 1 of these very large sachets would be fine.

Polenta with Gorgonzola

I love meals that are pulled together really casually and put on the table for everyone to help themselves. This polenta dish is one of them. Making polenta is a communal affair in our house: as someone stirs at the stove there is inevitably someone else sitting at the kitchen bench giving instructions, both participants with a glass in hand. Perfect Sunday night fare served with crusty bread and a salad.

1.25 litres milk
1 teaspoon salt
175 g polenta
80 g chilled unsalted butter
freshly ground black pepper
250–300 g gorgonzola

To make the polenta, bring the milk to a boil in a large saucepan and add the salt. Slowly pour in the polenta in a slow stream, stirring continuously with a wooden spoon. Once all the polenta has been added, turn down the heat. Continue stirring so that a skin does not form and the polenta does not catch on the bottom of the pan. Also, cooking the polenta slowly means it won't be bitter.

The polenta will be tender and pull away from the sides of the pan when it is cooked – this will take 40–50 minutes. Dice the chilled butter, then stir through the polenta and season with pepper.

Spoon the polenta into a deep serving dish to cover the base, then bring it up the sides, too. Add a layer of thickly sliced gorgonzola, then cover this with polenta. Continue layering and finish with a layer of gorgonzola. If the polenta is not hot enough to melt the cheese, place the dish briefly under a grill. For a simpler treatment, spoon the polenta onto a serving dish and top with thick slices of gorgonzola. Serve immediately. Serves 6–8

cooking polenta   It is a common mistake to undercook polenta – when it is ready it should not be 'tough' in any way, nor should it feel grainy in the mouth. At the 2001 Melbourne Food & Wine Festival Masterclass, I enjoyed watching Paul Wilson prepare a dish of truffled polenta and poached eggs. While the technique he used is not appropriate here, I was intrigued to learn that he cooked the polenta for 2 hours! It was silky-smooth and quite extraordinary. The simple recipe opposite doesn't need such attention, but please don't be tempted to rush cooking the polenta – take your time and savour the results.

The Butcher

When I first came to the Valley, it was in the butcher shops more than anywhere else that I noticed Barossa Deutsch was spoken, not so much from butcher to customer but between those waiting in the shop. Each butcher in each town had a smokehouse and a style of their own, and families would often go to one butcher for their lachsschinken, another for their mettwurst and yet another for their blood sausage. Sadly, this is rare these days, but there is no stronger representation of the culture the early settlers brought with them to South Australia in the mid-nineteenth century than the butcher shops of the Barossa. The German names still over the doors of these shops are testimony to this, as are the truly wonderful smallgoods.

My relationship with Schulz's of Angaston began when I first tasted their sugar-cured, double-smoked bacon. This bacon remains a passion, especially with just-cooked, free-range eggs with deep-golden yolks and a slab of Apex bread toasted and spread with lashings of unsalted butter. And, dare I say it, barbecue sauce on the side. The perfect Sunday breakfast and hangover cure!

My association with Schulz's has continued through various incarnations, from the original days of Bruce Schulz and then Vern, who took over the mantle for many years, Merv, the master smoker, and on to Steve and the boys there now. Vern, a big man with a barrel chest and ruddy cheeks, was the epitome of what a butcher should look like. He always wore a striped apron and scabbard, and even though he worked very long hours, he was always happy to oblige my strange requests, ordering almost any part of any animal, fresh or brined, or agreeing to smoke whole piglets, for example.

The strong tradition of the smokehouse is what first drew me to Schulz's. Merv understood its intricacies like no one else. Keeping a smokehouse going for

two to three days, no matter the weather, stoking up the fire at night so that the smoking continues until the fire is stirred again in the morning, is an art form. Whether I was wanting to experiment with cold-smoking kangaroo fillets or follow through an idea of my friend Cheong Liew, where hares were gutted and smoked in their skins (which resulted in the most wonderful, buttery flesh), Schulz's always helped me. When it came to trying the ham in hay recipe on page 314, I was confident that the flavour of a ham smoked at Schulz's would withstand the long soaking required to rid it of any excess salt before cooking. And so it did – beautifully.

Not so long ago, butchers worked on sawdust-strewn floors and cut up meat on marble slabs, methods now gone with revised hygiene practices and the introduction of quality-assurance schemes. But we still get old-fashioned good service in the Valley. I admit you can't be in too much of a hurry when you walk into a Barossa butcher, but that's part of the enjoyment for me. Youngsters are handed a piece of that South Australian speciality, bung fritz, a custom that has continued for generations, and there's always time to talk about what you want and how you plan to cook it.

While I am lucky enough to be able to look at a whole carcass before choosing what I want and how I'd like it cut up, it's really the spirit of Schulz's that keeps me going back. This is epitomised by the patience and gentleness I've seen displayed so often, particularly when an older customer is buying the smallest amount of meat imaginable. It's clear that these customers are as valued as those whose bills are considerable. Perhaps kindness is part of a butcher's psyche, but it must also be due in part to the fact that there is a real food culture in the Barossa. Dedication to good produce is always respected, no matter who you are.

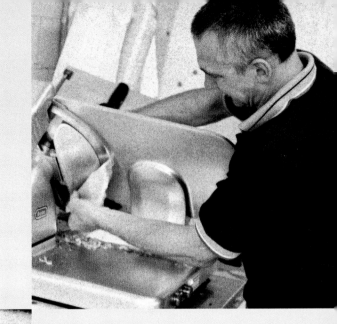

A.C. SCHULZ
LIMITED
BUTCHERS

MARINATED
LAMB
STEAKS
$8·99
K.C.

Squid Stuffed with Freekah, Green Olives and Preserved Lemon

Baking squid is a surefire way of avoiding overcooking it. Ask your fishmonger to clean the squid, but make sure you get the tentacles and that the outer membrane is left in place as this crazes during cooking, adding a pinkish tone and providing a natural sea flavour.

4 squid, cleaned (outer
  membrane left on)

freekah stuffing

190 g freekah (cracked or
  wholegrain) *or* burghul

500 ml chicken stock

reserved squid tentacles

2 cloves garlic

2 tablespoons extra-virgin
  olive oil

1 generous handful
  flat-leaf parsley

90 g green olives

2 tablespoons chopped
  preserved lemon

sea salt

freshly ground black pepper

To make the stuffing, bring the freekah and chicken stock to a boil in a saucepan and simmer gently for 10 minutes if cooking cracked grain or 25 minutes for wholegrain, or until just tender. Drain and set aside.

Finely chop the tentacles and garlic and sauté in the olive oil in a frying pan for 2 minutes. Roughly chop the parsley (you need about 1 cup) and slice the flesh away from the olives, then fold through the freekah with the preserved lemon and tentacles. Season with salt and pepper. Pack the stuffing into the squid tubes, leaving 2–3 cm at the top to allow the stuffing to swell during cooking. Secure the top of each squid with a metal skewer.

Preheat the oven to 240°C. Put the stuffed squid tubes into a large baking dish brushed with olive oil, leaving a good amount of space between each one. Brush more olive oil over the squid and bake for about 20 minutes or until opaque. Allow to rest upside-down for 5 minutes before slicing thickly.

The stuffed squid can also be cooked directly on the barbecue, but extra care needs to be taken when turning them so that they cook evenly and don't burn. **Serves 8**

freekah   Freekah is simply wheat that's been harvested green and then roasted. I use freekah that comes from the Adelaide Plains – look for it in gourmet food stores.

Mussels Grilled in the Shell with a Roasted Almond Salsa

This is a great way to cook mussels: they look and taste fantastic (see the photograph on page 38). I have to admit, however, that removing the top shell isn't particularly easy. If you want to avoid this job, stand the mussels over the fire until opened, then add the salsa and a drizzle of oil before serving.

3 kg black mussels

extra-virgin olive oil

roasted almond salsa

100 g almonds

2 cloves garlic

1 Meyer lemon

125 ml extra-virgin olive oil

½ teaspoon salt

½ teaspoon freshly ground
  black pepper

To make the salsa, preheat the oven to 220°C. Roast the almonds on a baking tray for about 5 minutes, shaking the tray to prevent the nuts from burning. Allow to cool, then grind coarsely in a food processor. Finely chop the garlic and slice the lemon finely before cutting it into small pieces. Mix all the salsa ingredients together in a bowl and set aside. The salsa can be made up to 12 hours in advance.

Heat the grill on a barbecue while preparing the mussels – if using a wood-fired grill, make sure the fire has burned down to a bed of glowing embers (using grapevine cuttings is helpful here as they burn quickly). Scrub and debeard the mussels, then, using a small paring knife, slide the tip of the knife between the shells and slide down to cut through the hinge, in much the same way as you shuck an oyster. Remove the top shell, taking care not to let any broken shell get on the mussel.

Spoon a little of the salsa on top of each mussel and drizzle with some extra-virgin olive oil. Grill for about 3 minutes – the mussels will poach in their own juices and are cooked when they become opaque. Serves 8–10

Fish Baked in Salt

Fish doesn't stand overcooking, but I have to admit that this method produces such a moist result that there is little room for error. The salt forms a crust on the skin during cooking, then you simply peel the skin away from the flesh with the salt. This method is perfect for when you catch a fish when you're on holidays and don't feel confident about scaling it.

1 × 1.75 kg snapper, cleaned

2 kg rock salt

4 quarters preserved lemon

3 large sprigs dill

Preheat the oven to 240°C. Wash the fish under cold running water and pat it dry with kitchen paper. Spread a quarter of the rock salt evenly in a deep baking dish.

Remove the flesh from the preserved lemon and rinse the rind well. Put the preserved lemon and dill inside the fish cavity and put the fish on the rock salt. Pile the remaining salt over the fish to cover it completely. Bake for 25 minutes. Remove the top layer of salt and serve. Serves 6

Salmon with Sorrel Butter

A filleted side of salmon or cutlets prepared by your fishmonger are the closest thing I know to convenience food that doesn't compromise quality or flavour. If the sorrel butter is waiting in the freezer, you can have a really smart dinner on the table in 5 minutes, and that includes making the green salad.

1 side of salmon (skin on)

extra-virgin olive oil

sea salt

freshly ground black pepper

sorrel butter

8 generous handfuls sorrel

225 g softened unsalted butter

1 teaspoon freshly ground
  black pepper

Remove the feather bones from the salmon with fish tweezers. Cut the salmon into approximately 6 × 200 g portions, but do not use the tail ends (use these in another dish). Remove the skin from the thinner, tail-end portions and reserve.

To make the sorrel butter, remove the stems from the sorrel and shred the leaves (you need 4 cups tightly packed sorrel). Melt 25 g of the butter in a frying pan, then sauté the sorrel until wilted. Put the sorrel into a sieve and press out as much liquid as possible. Leave to cool to room temperature. Blend the remaining butter, wilted sorrel and pepper in a food processor until the sorrel has been worked in completely and the butter is a deep olive-green.

Put a little olive oil into a non-stick or cast-iron frying pan and heat until almost smoking. Cook the salmon, skin-side down first, until almost cooked through. Turn and cook for another minute. Keep the fish warm while crisping the reversed fish skin in the pan. Serve the fish topped with a dollop of sorrel butter and a piece of crispy fish skin. **Serves 6**

Blond Liver Brochettes

Blond livers are found in mature chooks (although not always), which usually means that they have been free-ranged or corn-fed or both, as birds raised by other means tend to be slaughtered much younger. These livers are larger, creamier and more flavoursome, the very best of them being paler too, hence 'blond'. Having said all that, any fresh chicken livers can be used here.

500 g best-quality blond
  chicken livers
extra-virgin olive oil
12 fresh bay leaves *or*
  1 tablespoon lemon thyme
  leaves
12 shallots

Soak 4 large wooden skewers (or 6 smaller ones) in water for 30 minutes. Meanwhile, trim the livers, keeping only the large lobes. If using the lemon thyme rather than the bay leaves, drizzle ¼ cup extra-virgin olive oil over the livers and sprinkle with the lemon thyme, then leave for 30 minutes.

Meanwhile, peel the shallots, then boil them in water for 10 minutes and allow to cool enough to handle. Each shallot will break into 2 pieces, one larger than the other. Brush the shallots with a little olive oil.

Heat your barbecue thoroughly before you are ready to cook – if using wood, make sure the fire burns down to glowing embers. Assemble the skewers by starting with a bay leaf, if using, then a piece of onion, followed by a chicken liver. Fill all the skewers this way, then brush with a little olive oil.

Grill the brochettes for 2–3 minutes on the first side, then turn them over and grill for another 1–2 minutes, depending on how pink you like your liver. Allow to rest away from the heat for 5 minutes before serving. **Serves 4**

leftovers for lunch   These livers are lovely cold, if you've cooked too many. I had great success once with a salad of baby cos leaves, leftover slow-roasted tomatoes, witlof, avocado and the cold livers and shallots. Finished with a red-wine vinegar and extra-virgin olive oil dressing, it made a fantastic lunch.

Coq au Vin

Trying coq au vin a decade ago, I wondered what all the fuss was about. Now I know it's all about starting with a really good chook and decent wine (no vin ordinaire here, please), and allowing the time – for a peasant dish, this requires attention to detail. And, dare I say it, the finished result is outstanding. The sauce is so good you won't want to waste a drop.

1 × 2.6 kg free-range cockerel

  or chicken

18 mushrooms

2 carrots

2 sticks celery

100 g salt pork

1 tablespoon extra-virgin

  olive oil

40 g softened unsalted butter

24 pickling onions

2 sprigs thyme

5 fresh bay leaves

¼ cup brandy

375 ml very reduced veal stock

1 tablespoon unbleached

  plain flour

1 cup flat-leaf parsley leaves

marinade

2 cloves garlic

1 onion

2 sprigs thyme

750 ml red wine

Joint the cockerel or chicken by taking off the legs and separating the drumsticks from the thighs. 'French' the wings by cutting off the tips. Cut away the bottom part of the spine and reserve. Turn the bird over and cut through the cartilage that separates the breasts. Cut through the breast at an angle, so that the pieces are even (this will help make the cooking time as much the same as possible for each piece). To make the marinade, slice the garlic and onion and mix with the thyme and red wine in a large non-reactive bowl. Marinate the cockerel pieces overnight or for a minimum of 8 hours. Next day, remove the cockerel shortly before cooking and reserve the marinade.

Preheat the oven to 150°C. Peel the mushrooms and dice the carrots and celery, then set aside. Remove the rind from the salt pork and cut the meat into 2.5 cm cubes. Heat the olive oil and half the butter until foamy in a large ovenproof pot. Sauté the salt pork until browned and remove with a slotted spoon. Gently seal the cockerel pieces in the pot, taking care not to burn the butter. Remove and set aside. Toss the pickling onions in the butter until slightly coloured, then remove and set aside. Repeat this with the mushrooms, and set aside. Add the carrot, celery, thyme and bay leaves and cook until lightly caramelised.

Return the cockerel pieces to the pot, then gently stir through the carrot, celery and herbs. Warm the brandy in a small saucepan, then light it carefully with a match and wait for the alcohol to burn off, then pour it over the meat. Pour in the reduced stock and 375 ml of the reserved marinade and slowly bring to a simmer. Put the lid on the pot and cook in the oven for 1½ hours. Remove from the oven and cool completely before refrigerating.

Before serving, preheat the oven to 150°C. Remove the fat that has settled on the top of the coq au vin, then add the pickling onions and mushrooms. Reheat the dish in the oven, or warm it through on the stove for 30 minutes using a simmer pad. Strain the cooking liquor from the cockerel and cover the meat to keep it warm. Bring the cooking liquor to a boil and reduce the juices a little. Make a paste with the flour and remaining butter and whisk small amounts into the sauce over heat to thicken it. Simmer for a further 10 minutes until lightly thickened with a glossy sheen. Pour the sauce over the cockerel, sprinkle with the parsley and serve. **Serves 6**

Pheasant with Apple, Calvados and Cream

All my pheasant dishes are cooked with young birds as I've always had farmed birds to hand. In Europe the wild bird is of indeterminate age and any recipes from there take this into account. Here I use the flavour principles from a Normandy recipe in Elizabeth David's *French Provincial Cooking*, but have changed the method entirely to suit young birds.

2 × 800 g pheasants

1 tablespoon extra-virgin
  olive oil

20 g butter

1 lemon

2 large apples

4 sprigs marjoram

⅓ cup Calvados

250 ml reduced golden
  chicken stock

250 ml rich cream

marinade

2 tablespoons extra-virgin
  olive oil

1 tablespoon freshly chopped
  marjoram

freshly ground black pepper

Joint the pheasants by cutting each bird in two down the spine, leaving the legs attached to the bone and the breasts also on the bone. Combine the marinade ingredients and rub into the pheasant, then cover and leave for 1 hour.

In a heavy-based, deep pot with a lid, heat the olive oil and butter until foaming. Very gently seal the pheasant until light golden in colour. Make sure you do this slowly, and turn the pieces over constantly, so neither the meat nor skin 'seizes' or contracts, which will make the pheasant tough.

Remove the zest from the lemon in wide strips using a potato peeler, and peel and quarter the apples. Add the zest, apple and marjoram to the pot and pour in the Calvados. Heat gently, then touch a match to the surface of the Calvados to burn off the alcohol. Add the chicken stock and cream and very gently bring to a slow simmer. Put the pot on a simmer pad, cover with the lid and cook slowly for 30 minutes.

Remove the pheasant from the cooking liquor, then cover it so that it keeps warm while resting. Bring the liquor to a boil and cook until slightly thickened.

To serve, carve the breast off the bone and the legs off the spine and separate the thigh from the drumstick. Bone out the thigh bone and slice the meat into 3 pieces. Put a breast, some sliced thigh meat and a drumstick on each warmed plate, along with 2 pieces of apple per person. Spoon over a little of the sauce and serve immediately. Serves 4

new york dressed   If it's possible to buy pheasant in feather with the guts in (New York dressed), then age it for a week in the refrigerator before cooking to add another dimension to the flavour.

Double-cut Grilled Lemon Thyme Chops

I love barbecuing really thick lamb chops, so I ask the butcher to cut them at least double thickness. Short-loin chops 3 cm thick give me that desirable effect of a frizzled fatty tail and meat that's pink and moist in the middle and charcoaled on the outside. One per person is enough, but then, they are *so* sweet and juicy, and as there's often nothing more than a salad and crusty bread at a barbecue . . .

4 double-cut lamb loin chops

salt

lemon thyme marinade

2 lemons

2 tablespoons lemon juice

125 ml extra-virgin olive oil

2 tablespoons lemon thyme
  leaves

freshly ground black pepper

To make the marinade, slice 1 lemon finely and mix with half the lemon juice, half the olive oil and half the lemon thyme in a flat glass dish. Put the chops into the marinade 20 minutes before cooking, turning them to coat, then grind on black pepper. Cover with plastic film. Turn the chops over several times during the 20 minutes.

Meanwhile, prepare the barbecue – it must be very hot. (When we cook these chops over an open fire we let the fire burn down to red-hot embers that are covered with ash.) Remove the chops from the marinade and transfer them to the grill. It's best to turn them several times during cooking to minimise burning, beginning with 3 minutes on the first side so that the meat seals (turn it any earlier than this and the flesh will stick to the grill). Season the meat with salt just before turning it the first time. My chops are usually about 4 cm thick and take about 8 minutes to cook. This method produces medium–rare meat.

Make a fresh batch of marinade with the remaining ingredients and rest the grilled chops in this for about 10 minutes. Serve with boiled waxy potatoes and a salad. **Serves 4**

Treasure's Lamb and Pickled Quince Pies

We have these pies on the menu at the Farm Shop through most of winter, courtesy of Trevor (aka Treasure) Cook. We use Saskia's milk-fed lamb mostly as she finds it difficult selling the shoulder; while we are doing her a good turn, it also produces a great pie with the addition of the pickled quince. We freeze the uncooked pies and then cook them to order – an added bonus.

extra-virgin olive oil

1 kg diced shoulder of lamb

1 large onion

2 cloves garlic

100 g butter

sea salt

freshly ground black pepper

1 tablespoon unbleached
  plain flour

3 teaspoons tomato paste

1 fresh bay leaf

1 sprig thyme

1 sprig rosemary

100 ml red wine

50 ml red-wine vinegar

500 ml lamb *or* veal stock

1 quantity Sour Cream Pastry
  (page 127)

100 g Flo Beer's Pickled
  Quince (page 182)

2 tablespoons freshly chopped
  flat-leaf parsley

1 free-range egg

¼ cup milk

Heat a splash of olive oil in a large, heavy-based pot and seal small quantities of the meat at a time until golden, then tip the meat onto a plate and wipe out the pot.

Chop the onion and garlic. Heat the butter and a spoonful of olive oil in the pot, then add the onion and garlic and cook until caramelised. Add the sealed lamb and season. Stand the pot over medium heat, then add the flour, tomato paste, bay leaf and chopped thyme and rosemary, stirring well. Turn up the heat and deglaze the pan with the wine and vinegar, then add the stock and reduce the temperature to low to medium. Cook until tender – this will depend on the age and quality of the meat. (For milk-fed lamb, 25 minutes will be perfect; if mutton is used, the meat will take 1½ hours and will be best if cooked even more slowly.) Remove from the stove and allow to cool.

Meanwhile, make and chill the pastry as instructed. I use a large muffin tin when making these pies, although smaller pies could also be made. Roll the chilled pastry out until 5 mm thick and cut out 6 rounds slightly larger than the diameter of a hole in the muffin tray – these are the pie lids. With the remaining pastry, cut out larger rounds to line the holes in the muffin tray, taking the pastry over the edge of each to form a lip.

Dice the pickled quince and stir it into the cooled lamb mixture with the parsley, then fill the pastry cases. Whisk the egg and milk together and brush this over the pastry 'lip'. Put the lids into position and press around the edges with a fork to seal. Using a sharp paring knife, trim the pastry and make a tiny hole in the top of each pie to allow steam to escape.

Refrigerate the pies while preheating the oven to 220°C. Brush the tops of the pies with the egg wash again and bake for 20 minutes. Reduce the heat to 180°C and bake for a further 25 minutes. Allow the pies to cool slightly before turning out. **Makes 6**

Smoked Lamb's Brains with Sorrel Mayonnaise

I can never resist brains on a menu, but Colin can't bear the thought of them. Our daughters love brains too, so I devised this dish in a bid to involve Colin as he enjoys using our little smoker. The creamy, smoked brains are so irresistible I think we nearly have him. Clever Damien Pignolet gave me the idea of soaking the brains in verjuice.

6 sets fresh lamb's brains

250 ml verjuice

4 slices rolled pancetta

55 g walnuts

4 generous handfuls sorrel

50 g butter

freshly ground black pepper

sorrel mayonnaise

2 handfuls sorrel

2 × 55 g free-range egg yolks

pinch of salt

½ lemon

125 ml mellow extra-virgin
  olive oil

125 ml grapeseed oil

sea salt

freshly ground black pepper

cold water (optional)

To make the mayonnaise, remove the stems from the sorrel and shred the leaves (you need 1 cup shredded leaves). Blend the egg yolks in a food processor or blender with the sorrel, salt and a squeeze of lemon juice. Combine the two oils, then, with the motor running, slowly add the oil to the sorrel mixture in a thin stream until the mixture becomes thick. Season with salt and pepper. If the mayonnaise is too thick, adjust with a little cold water.

Rinse the brains under cold water and blot dry with kitchen paper. Leave to soak in the verjuice in a non-reactive bowl for 30 minutes.

Meanwhile, prepare the smoker. Remove the brains from the verjuice and pat dry with kitchen paper. Put the brains top-side down on the rack in the smoker and smoke for 8 minutes. Turn and smoke for a further 5 minutes. Transfer the brains to a plate, then cover with plastic film and allow to cool.

Preheat the oven to 220°C. Put the pancetta on one baking tray and the walnuts on another, and transfer both to the oven for about 5 minutes. Shake the walnut tray to prevent the nuts from burning. If they are not fresh season's, rub the walnuts in a clean tea towel to remove the bitter skins. Allow to cool, then roughly chop. Crumble the pancetta and set aside.

Check the sorrel for any thick stalks and discard these, then wash and dry the sorrel thoroughly. To serve, divide the sorrel leaves between serving plates and scatter with the walnuts and crumbled pancetta. Place dollops of the mayonnaise on either side of each plate

Cut each set of brains in half through the cross-section. Heat the butter in a frying pan until nut-brown, then gently pan-fry the brains until a light golden colour. Put the brains on the salad, then season with pepper and serve immediately. Serves 4

Roasted Saltbush Mutton

There is nothing like proper saltbush mutton. I am lucky enough to have learnt how to cook it from Kerry Urry, who has grown up with it and whose butcher at Burra sources the real stuff, where saltbush is the main component of the sheep's diet. I like to hang a leg of saltbush mutton in my meat safe (see opposite), if the weather permits, to let its already unique flavour mature.

250 ml port

1 × 3.5 kg leg of saltbush
  mutton

extra-virgin olive oil

4 cloves garlic

4 sprigs rosemary

sea salt

freshly ground black pepper

Preheat the oven to 180°C. Gently warm half the port in a small non-reactive saucepan. Rinse the leg of lamb under running cold water, then dry it well and put it into a lightly oiled baking dish. Cut tiny pockets into the meat, then thickly slice the garlic and poke these into the meat. Pour the warm port over the leg. Strip the rosemary leaves from the stalks and scatter over the meat. Season with salt and pepper.

Bake the leg for 2 hours, basting it with the cooking juices every 30 minutes. Warm the remaining port and pour it over the leg, then return the meat to the oven for a further 2½ hours. (The fat content of mutton keeps the meat moist but makes it more susceptible to burning. It is important to watch that the juices do not burn in the bottom of the baking dish, as they will become bitter and taint the overall flavour. If this happens, you will need to change or clean the dish and return the meat to the oven for the balance of the cooking time.) Remove the meat from the oven and rest it, covered, for at least 20 minutes before carving. Serves 8–10

Pickled Pork with Pickled Quince

This is the meal that my late mother-in-law served when welcoming me into her family. It's such an important Beer dish that it finds its way onto my table in any season. As Flo would have known, the pork must be fatty or you shouldn't bother. You don't have to eat all the fat, but without it you won't have the flavour. The pickled quince saves the dish from being too rich.

1 × 1.3 kg hand of pickled
  pork

3.5 litres water

250 ml white-wine vinegar

2 onions

1 teaspoon black *or* white
  peppercorns

2 fresh bay leaves

12 pieces Flo Beer's Pickled
  Quince (page 182) *or* other
  pickled fruit

Put the pickled pork into a heavy-based non-reactive pot and pour in the water and vinegar. Peel and quarter the onions and add to the pot with the peppercorns and bay leaves, then bring to a simmer. Stand the pot on a simmer pad and simmer very slowly for 3 hours. Allow the pork to cool in the cooking liquor.

To serve, slice the meat and arrange it on a platter with the onion, a little of the cooking liquor and the pickled quince. **Serves 6**

hot or cold   Delicious hot, this is also good served cold (some would even say better), which means that it is always included in the line-up at Christmas in our house. A truly trans-seasonal dish.

My Italian Beef 'Daube'

Whenever I cook this dish, I am aware of the sweetness beef shin can produce, yet this 'lesser' cut is so often ignored. My friend Ann Parronchi took me to the terracotta kilns in Chianti where workmen used to cook beef shin overnight in the residual heat of the kiln. This is my interpretation of what that dish may have been like.

1 beef shin (off the bone)

2 sticks celery

1 carrot

1 onion

1 small leek

6 sprigs thyme

4 stalks parsley

1 bay leaf

800 ml veal stock

400 ml red wine

softened unsalted butter

unbleached plain flour

800 g shallots

2 quorms garlic

1 orange

1 cup kalamata olives

sea salt

freshly ground black pepper

marinade

1 orange

250–500 ml extra-virgin
  olive oil

1 fresh bay leaf

1 sprig rosemary

1 sprig thyme

several parsley stalks

To make the marinade, remove the zest from the orange with a potato peeler in one long strip, if possible. Pour the olive oil into a large glass container or a non-reactive pot and add the zest and herbs.

Remove all sinew and excess fat from the beef shin, then steep the beef in the olive oil and allow to marinate overnight (if marinating during the day, turn the meat frequently to make sure it remains moist and evenly exposed to the flavourings).

Remove the shin from the pot. Using a little of the oil from the marinade, gently seal the shin in a frying pan, then transfer the meat to a large, heavy-based pot. Dice the celery and carrot, and roughly chop the onion. Discard the green parts of the leek and chop the white part. Tip the chopped vegetables into the pot. Tie the thyme and parsley into a bundle with kitchen string and add to the pot with the bay leaf. Cover with the veal stock and red wine and bring to a simmer. Turn the heat down to a very gentle simmer, then cover with the lid and cook for 8 hours on top of the stove, turning several times. (You can also cook it in the oven at 140°C for the same length of time.) This is a large piece of mature meat and it needs to be cooked until it is tender to the touch and the sinews are like jelly.

The cooking juices will benefit from being reduced and thickened. Make a paste with equal quantities of butter and flour – you will need 30 g paste to every 250 ml cooking juices. Remove the meat from the cooking liquor and set aside covered (this helps retain its moistness). Bring the pot back to a fast simmer and reduce the juices a little. Slowly whisk in the paste in small amounts to thicken the sauce. Reduce the heat to a slow simmer and return the meat to the pot.

Meanwhile, preheat the oven to 200°C. Peel the shallots and the cloves of one of the quorms of garlic, then cut the remaining quorm in half through the middle. Melt a knob of butter in a large ovenproof pot. Add the shallots and all the garlic and toss to coat. Transfer the pot to the oven and roast until the shallots and garlic have caramelised, about 30 minutes. Set aside.

An hour before the daube is due to finish cooking, remove the zest from the orange with a potato peeler and add to the pot with the olives, shallots and garlic. When cooked, season the daube and serve in a warmed dish with polenta or mashed potato. Serves 6–8

crockpots   I've actually had most success with this dish when I've transferred the meat and its juices to a crockpot for the second cooking phase. The slow cooking in the crockpot produces a really luscious mouthfeel. On one occasion I cooked the meat in its juices for 1 hour on the higher crockpot setting, turning the meat over once, and then I reduced the heat to low and cooked it for a further 8 hours. Another time I started out in a cast-iron pot and after 3 hours in the second cooking transferred the meat and its sauce to the crockpot for the remaining time. I haven't done it, but my feeling is that the meat would be ready after 10–12 hours if cooked from start to finish in the crockpot.

Grilled Rib-eye Steaks with Anchovy Butter

I was brought up on the best back-cut rump steaks with a good selvage of fat, and my father taught me to cook them at a high temperature and then to rest them. Exhaust fans were unknown in those days, and the house would fill with smoke! Today, I prefer to do my grilling on the barbecue over hot coals, and especially love these rib-eyes on the bone.

4 × 5 cm thick rib-eye steaks

extra-virgin olive oil

2 tablespoons freshly chopped

  rosemary

1 teaspoon finely chopped

  garlic

sea salt

freshly ground black pepper

anchovy butter

250 g softened unsalted butter

30 anchovy fillets

1 teaspoon freshly ground

  black pepper

Rub the steaks with olive oil and season with the rosemary and garlic, then refrigerate.

To make the anchovy butter, blend all ingredients in a food processor until the anchovy fillets are finely chopped and well dispersed through the butter. Spoon the butter onto a piece of aluminium foil and roll into a log, twisting the ends to secure. Chill until firm.

Heat a clean barbecue grill until hot – if using a wood-fired grill, make sure the fire burns down to glowing embers. Season the steaks and then cook them for 4 minutes on one side. Turn and cook for another 4 minutes. Top each steak with half the anchovy butter and allow to rest in a warm spot for 10 minutes.

Just before serving, add a slice of the remaining anchovy butter to each steak. Serves 4

Pot-roasted Tongue with Pickled Plums and Sorrel Rémoulade

If you are feeding a tentative offal eater, this dish will confirm a real interest by taking the tongue to the second stage I've suggested. It is cooked slowly until really tender, then slices are pan-fried gently in nut-brown butter to caramelise the surface. Served with pickled plums and a dollop of the rémoulade, this is a startling dish.

1 ox tongue

1.5 litres water

1 onion

1 fresh bay leaf

½ teaspoon black peppercorns

1 quantity Sorrel Rémoulade
 (page 192)

Pickled Plums (page 16)

Put the tongue into a crockpot or cast-iron pot with a lid and cover with the water. Add the onion, bay leaf and peppercorns. If using a crockpot, cook the tongue gently for 8 hours or overnight; if using a cast-iron pot, cook it for the same time but stand the pot on a simmer pad over a very low heat.

When cooked, leave the tongue to cool slightly, and peel while still warm. Slice thickly – the most tender and delicious meat comes from the back of the tongue. Serve with a dollop of rémoulade and some pickled plums to the side.

If the cooked tongue has been refrigerated, it can be sliced and warmed in nut-brown butter in a frying pan. Remove the tongue from the pan and keep it warm, then add a little of the pickling syrup from the plums to the pan and reduce this to make a glossy sauce. Serves 6

The Pheasant Farm

PEACH AND WILD LIME Jam $6·50 MAGGIE BEER

MAGGIE BEER

BAROSSA CHRISTMAS PUDDING 900g NET

The Farm Shop at the Pheasant Farm is where it all began in 1979. It was here we realised we needed to show the public what they could do with the pheasants we were producing. The shop grew to become the Pheasant Farm Restaurant, which ruled our lives until late 1993.

The siting of the shop on the edge of our huge dam was a masterstroke, although this was due more to good luck than anything else. For a long time the dam was more like a moon crater, a blot on the landscape, but today it is surrounded by mature trees and filled with reeds that attract wild ducks, grebes, divers and snake-necked turtles. The surviving callop (yellow belly) have grown so large that they can be spotted easily in the deep water that changes from a crystal-clear blue in winter to green in summer, but without the murkiness you might expect from a dam.

In the early years we lived in what is now part of the Farm Shop. The most beautiful times were in winter when the fog rolled across the dam, making it feel for all the world like we were in the Highlands of Scotland. In summer, the sun setting on the Barossa hills behind would cast pinky-mauve reflections on the water, as it still does now. In those days we'd swim during the heatwaves and our daughters would catch yabbies through the cracks in the decking outside their bedroom, or they'd ride their ponies bareback into the water. It was a pretty idyllic existence, except for the pressure of Colin and me having to work every weekend.

Now we have come full circle and the Farm Shop has regained its original status. It must be remembered that the Pheasant Farm is first and foremost a farm, and the shop is part of that. Our first olive grove is here, as is the quince orchard, and there are always pheasants, guinea fowl or partridge on the go, no matter the season. Lush vineyards lie on one side of the river, which, flanked by huge river red gums, seldom runs.

There's no luxury of mains water here – even the dam is kept topped up by a bore. In the heat of summer our approach is down the driest, dustiest and bumpiest road you might encounter; in winter, it is muddy and just as bumpy. Best of all, until you are actually inside the Farm Shop, you have no idea what awaits on the other side: down the track, in the door, and there is that beautiful, tranquil dam – so very special in our dry climate.

While the Farm Shop is the public face of Maggie Beer Products, I like to see it more as being the end of the value-adding chain (the photographs opposite show some of its aspects, and the wonderful Jane Renner who runs it). Our products are certainly all available for tasting, but we also use the shop to take advantage of any local produce in peak condition that might make up a short run. These one-off items are produced in the kitchen on site, rather than in our Export Kitchen, where the commercial cooking is usually undertaken. These 'practice' runs give me the greatest pleasure – we might end up taking a great idea from a small run to a larger production, or we may simply be making the most of what's to hand. Whatever the case, we are always using local produce. As an example, I've just finished dehydrating Moya prune plums, using a method I saw in France last year. The farmer who grew these plums is tempted to pull his trees out as the local market isn't much interested. I can't wait to show him the prunes, in the hope I can convince him otherwise – their flavour is so exciting!

Every time I walk in the door of the Farm Shop I feel I am coming home, and I hope I never lose that joy. While life elsewhere just gets busier, we often visit for breakfast on the weekend simply to enjoy the quiet by the dam, to feel at peace with the world and to reflect on what's been and what's to come.

Olive Oil Brioche

While reading Patricia Wells's *At Home in Provence* I came across a recipe for an olive oil brioche flavoured with citrus zest, a wonderful extension of the more usual buttery version. I have taken the idea a little further for the very specific reason of creating a brioche to serve toasted with my pâté, and use a very fruity, almost green oil to balance the zest, which I've doubled.

15 g fresh *or* 1½ teaspoons
  dried yeast

1½ teaspoons castor sugar

250 ml lukewarm water

¼ cup extra-virgin olive oil

3 × 55 g free-range eggs

grated zest of 2 oranges

grated zest of 2 lemons

675 g unbleached strong flour

3 teaspoons salt

1 free-range egg yolk

1 tablespoon milk

In the bowl of an electric mixer fitted with a dough hook, mix the yeast, castor sugar and lukewarm water. Set aside for 5–10 minutes until frothy. Add the olive oil, eggs and zests and stir to combine.

Mix the flour and salt, then add a little at a time to the yeast mixture with the dough hook on low speed until it has all been combined and the dough starts to form a ball. Turn the dough out onto a floured bench and knead for 10 minutes until soft and satiny, adding a little extra flour if it becomes too sticky. Return the dough to the bowl and cover tightly with plastic film, then refrigerate for 12 hours until doubled in volume.

Remove the dough from the refrigerator and allow it to return to room temperature (this will take about 1 hour). Knead the dough lightly for a minute or two, then divide it into 2 portions and put these into loaf tins or large brioche moulds. (This dough does not need to be knocked back – doughs with a higher fat content struggle to rise again if knocked back.) Leave to rise in a draught-free spot for about 40 minutes until half the volume again.

Preheat the oven to 220°C. Mix the egg yolk with the milk and brush this over the tops of the loaves. Bake for 10 minutes, then reduce the temperature to 180°C and bake for a further 20 minutes. Turn the loaves out onto a wire rack and allow to cool. **Makes 2**

Sweet Biscuits with Blood-orange Icing

These biscuits were totally unplanned. During a photo shoot for this book, my publisher Julie Gibbs was in a playful mood, having bought biscuit cutters from Mavis Kraft's shop in Tanunda for Zöe, Max and Lily. Down came my old cookbooks, and once we'd established a flour/butter/liquid ratio, we were soon rolling and cutting the dough, which was enriched with cream and eggs by Sophie.

450 g unbleached plain flour

1 teaspoon baking powder

55 g icing sugar

55 g unsalted butter

2 × 55 g free-range egg yolks

120 ml cream

icing

100 g icing sugar

2 teaspoons blood-orange *or*
   lemon juice

To make the biscuits, sift the dry ingredients into a large mixing bowl and rub in the butter with your fingertips. Make a well in the centre. Whisk the egg yolks and cream together and pour into the well. With a fork, slowly incorporate the flour and egg yolk mixtures. Turn the dough out onto a lightly floured bench and gently knead for 2 minutes until smooth. Refrigerate for 15 minutes.

Preheat the oven to 180°C. Roll out the dough until 3 mm thick, then, using biscuit cutters, cut out shapes and transfer these to a baking tray lined with baking paper. Reform the dough and roll and cut it again. Bake the biscuits for 20–25 minutes, until lightly golden. Allow to cool on a wire rack before icing.

To make the icing, sift the icing sugar into a bowl and mix in the blood-orange or lemon juice. If the mixture is a little stiff, warm it in the microwave or in a saucepan until it's a spreadable consistency. Using a spatula or flat-bladed knife, spread a thin layer of icing over each biscuit and leave to dry. Store in an air-tight container once set. Makes 15–20

icing   While blood-orange icing is given here, we also iced the biscuits with a simple lemon icing (as shown in the photograph on page 241), which was delicious, too. The biscuits would be equally good with vanilla or passionfruit icing. In fact, ice these with whatever flavour you fancy!

Tiny Chocolate and Seville Paste Tarts

I developed Seville paste, one of our smaller commercial lines, to serve with blue cheese after hearing from my friend Will Studd that he had been given a slab of perfectly ripe Stilton with marmalade by Randolph Hodgson of Neale's Yard Dairy in London. Great as Seville paste is with blue cheese, when you combine it with a good couverture chocolate it is sensational.

1 quantity Sour Cream Pastry
  (page 127)

filling
500 g Haigh's couverture
  chocolate
170 ml double cream
1 small tub Maggie Beer's
  Seville Paste

Make and chill the pastry as instructed. Roll the chilled pastry out until about 3 mm thick, then cut rounds large enough to fit over the base of a small glass (an espresso glass is ideal, although I also use others). Stand the upturned glasses on a baking tray and drape a pastry round over the base of each one, as illustrated on page 240. Gently mould the pastry around the base to form a 'cup'. Refrigerate for 20 minutes.

Meanwhile, preheat the oven to 200°C. Bake the pastry cases on the upturned glasses for 30–40 minutes, until golden. Remove the cases from the glasses and return the cases, right-side up, to the oven on the baking tray for another 10 minutes. Transfer the pastry cases to a wire rack to cool.

To make the filling, bring a saucepan of water to a boil. Roughly chop the couverture chocolate and put it into a mixing bowl with the cream. Turn the heat off under the saucepan, but leave the pan in place. Stand the bowl over the pan of hot water and allow the chocolate to melt slowly into the cream. Gently stir with a wooden spoon to combine, then allow to cool.

Pour a little of the cooled chocolate into the pastry cases to cover the base of each, then allow to cool. For each tart, take ½ teaspoon Seville paste and roll it into a ball. Put a ball of paste into the middle of each tart. Spoon in more of the chocolate to bring the level to just above the paste, and leave to set at room temperature. There is a photograph of these tarts on page 241. **Makes 15–25**

haigh's   I use South Australian products whenever I can and love Haigh's chocolate. There's a great story here: in 1950 John Haigh set out from Adelaide for Switzerland and worked his way into the heart of the Lindt family factory to learn their secrets. The influence of John Haigh's Swiss experience is still felt today. I recently held a blind-tasting of Lindt, Belgian and Haigh's couverture chocolate and was so impressed by the Haigh's that I now use it exclusively.

Blood-orange Tartlets

The idea for these tartlets came about by thinking about lemon curd and ending up at the blood orange, but it could extend to any other citrus. Pink grapefruit, mandarin, tangelo curd – I can taste them all, but nothing could topple the depth of colour from the blood orange. The flavour of this curd relies on the zest, so don't take any shortcuts. Any leftovers are great on toast for breakfast!

1 quantity Sour Cream Pastry
  (page 127)
3 blood oranges

blood-orange curd
130 g unsalted butter
180 g castor sugar
4 × 55 g free-range eggs
110 ml freshly squeezed and
  strained blood-orange juice

Make and chill the pastry as instructed. Roll the chilled pastry out until about 3 mm thick, then cut rounds large enough to fit over the base of a small glass (an espresso glass is ideal, although I also use others). Stand the upturned glasses on a baking tray and drape a pastry round over the base of each one, as illustrated below. Gently mould the pastry around the base to form a 'cup'. Refrigerate for 20 minutes.

Meanwhile, preheat the oven to 200°C. Bake the pastry cases on the upturned glasses for 30–40 minutes, until golden. Remove the cases from the glasses and return the cases, right-side up, to the oven on the baking tray for another 10 minutes. Transfer the pastry cases to a wire rack to cool.

To make the blood-orange curd, bring a saucepan of water to a boil and put the butter and castor sugar into a mixing bowl. Turn the water down to a simmer, then stand the bowl over the pan and stir to dissolve the sugar. Whisk the eggs into the butter mixture, then the orange juice. Using a wooden spoon, stir the mixture well over a gentle heat until it thickens. This will take 15–25 minutes. Allow to cool, then refrigerate.

Remove the zest from the blood oranges and set aside. Cut the segments away with a sharp paring knife to leave all pith and membrane behind, then put the segments into a small bowl. Squeeze the remaining juice from the membrane over the segments – this helps keep the fruit moist and means you don't lose any of that glorious colour.

Put a spoonful of orange curd into each tart base, then top with 2–3 orange segments, as shown opposite. Sprinkle the tartlets with a little zest and serve. Makes 15–25

Sophie's Apple Tea Cake with Caramelised Verjuice Syrup

When I was preparing the manuscript for *Cooking with Verjuice*, I asked several close friends and colleagues to reminisce about their experiences with verjuice and to include a favourite recipe. This tea cake comes from Sophie Zalokar, mentioned often through this book and, interestingly, the only person to provide a sweet offering. As ever, her use of ingredients is intuitive and the result divine.

6 small golden delicious apples

castor sugar

250 ml verjuice

¾ teaspoon ground cassia

cake

100 g softened unsalted butter

100 g castor sugar

2 × 61 g free-range eggs

250 g unbleached plain flour

1 teaspoon bicarbonate of soda

1 teaspoon cream of tartar

½ teaspoon salt

125 ml milk

1 teaspoon pure vanilla extract

caramelised verjuice syrup

250 ml verjuice

240 g castor sugar

300 ml reserved apple cooking
  syrup

Peel and core the apples, then cut them into eighths and put them into a saucepan with ¼ cup castor sugar and the verjuice. Bring to a boil over a high heat, then gently stir until the sugar has dissolved. Turn off the heat but don't move the pan. Leave the apple in this light syrup for 10 minutes, then drain, reserving the syrup (you should have about 300 ml).

Preheat the oven to 180°C and grease and line a 22 cm springform tin. To make the cake, cream the butter and castor sugar until pale and thick. Add the eggs one at a time, beating well after each addition. (If the mixture starts to curdle, add a tablespoon of the measured flour to stabilise it.) Sift the flour, bicarbonate of soda, cream of tartar and salt and add alternately to the egg mixture with the milk and vanilla extract. Spoon the batter into the prepared tin and smooth the top.

Arrange the apple on the top in a concentric pattern, pushing the pieces into the batter slightly. Mix 2 teaspoons castor sugar and the ground cassia and sprinkle evenly over the top. Bake for 45 minutes or until a skewer inserted into the centre of the cake comes out clean. Let the cake stand in the tin for at least 10 minutes, then remove the tin carefully.

While the cake is cooking, make the syrup. Have iced water ready in the sink or a large bowl. Bring the verjuice and castor sugar to a boil in a saucepan and cook until a deep, golden brown. Remove the caramel from the heat and cautiously add the reserved apple cooking syrup – the mixture may spit a little. Stand the saucepan in the iced water immediately to arrest the cooking, then pour into a jug ready to serve.

To serve, brush the warm cake with the syrup. Put a wedge of warm cake onto each plate (one with a gentle lip is best), then ladle over the syrup and offer with a hearty dollop of thick cream.

Serves 8

Lemon Delicious Puddings

There are no secrets about this old-fashioned pudding. What I am proud of, however, is that we make it commercially from our Export Kitchen at Tanunda with the exact same care as you would in your own kitchen, down to zesting the fresh lemons and breaking the free-range eggs. This may seem unremarkable, but it's most unusual on a large scale. Do what we do and find the best ingredients you can.

3 lemons

60 g softened unsalted butter

200 g castor sugar

3 large free-range eggs

60 g self-raising flour

350 ml milk

Preheat the oven to 100°C and lightly grease 8 dariole moulds. Finely grate the lemons to remove the zest, then juice them (you need ⅓ cup juice). Cream the butter and castor sugar in an electric mixer until pale and thick. Separate the eggs, then beat the egg yolks into the butter mixture until blended. Add the flour and milk slowly, beginning with a little flour, then some milk, and so on. Add the lemon juice and zest and mix to a smooth batter.

Whisk the egg whites until light and fluffy, then gently fold into the batter. Pour the batter into the dariole moulds, leaving space for the puddings to rise during cooking. Stand the moulds in a baking dish and pour hot water to come two-thirds of the way up their sides, then cover the dish tightly with greased foil. Bake for 1 hour, then turn off the oven, leaving the puddings inside so that they settle rather than collapse.

These puddings turn out beautifully, and are luscious served with some runny cream and extra lemon zest. Makes 8

Burnt Tangelo Cream

Sophie put this together after we had been reminiscing about the Pheasant Farm days. It's unbelievably luscious but very, very rich and needs to be served with a light accompaniment, such as a citrus salad. To make this salad, simply toss the segments and zest of a variety of citrus fruit – tangelos, grapefruit, oranges and limes, for example.

5 tangelos

110 g castor sugar

600 ml cream

2 × 55 g free-range eggs

4 × 55 g free-range egg yolks

Preheat the oven to 180°C. Remove the zest from 3 of the tangelos, then juice all 5 (you need 500 ml). Bring the zest, juice and castor sugar to a boil in a non-reactive saucepan. Stir to dissolve the sugar. Boil the syrup until it caramelises to a deep-amber colour. Stir in the cream until blended and remove from the heat.

Whisk the eggs and egg yolks in a bowl, then whisk in the caramel. Strain this custard through a fine sieve into a 1 litre ceramic serving bowl. Stand the bowl in a baking dish and pour in hot water to come two-thirds of the way up the sides of the bowl, then bake for 45 minutes until set with a slight crust. Remove the bowl from the water bath and allow to cool, then refrigerate.

Spoon the chilled tangelo cream out onto serving plates and partner with citrus salad, if desired. **Serves 12**

Rhubarb and Blood-orange Crumble

There is a bit of an art to making crumble: if you don't mix all the ingredients with your fingertips until crumbly with tiny buttery lumps it will be gluggy after cooking. I happen to think that almost any fruit 'crumbles' well, but rhubarb cooked in blood-orange juice and zest is probably the most startling of all, both in colour and intensity of flavour.

8 stalks rhubarb

3 blood oranges

50 g softened unsalted butter

2 tablespoons castor sugar

crumble

360 g unbleached plain flour

1 teaspoon baking powder

1 teaspoon ground cassia

180 g castor sugar

250 g chilled unsalted butter

1 teaspoon pure vanilla extract

To make the crumble, sift the flour, baking powder and ground cassia into a bowl and add the castor sugar. Dice the butter, then rub it and the vanilla extract into the flour with your fingertips until the mixture is crumbly and lumpy.

Wash the rhubarb, then discard the leaves and chop the stalks into 3 cm lengths. Remove the zest from the blood oranges and set aside, then cut the orange segments away with a sharp paring knife to leave all pith and membrane behind. Butter a medium-sized baking dish with most of the softened butter, leaving a little to dot over the fruit. Put the rhubarb, orange segments and zest into the dish, then dot with the remaining butter and sprinkle over the castor sugar.

Preheat the oven to 200°C. Generously pile the crumble over the fruit. The rhubarb will collapse when cooked, so it is important to cover the fruit thickly. Bake for 45–60 minutes, until the crumble is golden brown and the juice from the fruit is bubbling around the edges. Serve with double cream. Serves 6–8

Steamed Cumquat and Almond Pudding with Candied Cumquats

I love the flavour of cumquats, and often turn to the trees growing in tubs in my courtyard (it doesn't take much reflection to understand how much I love bitter flavours). This steamed pudding is a very grown-up affair, and while I seldom set the time aside to make such a dessert, this one is the exception.

softened unsalted butter

unbleached plain flour

55 g almonds

120 g castor sugar

1 tablespoon finely grated
  orange zest

2 × 55 g free-range eggs

½ teaspoon salt

½ teaspoon ground cassia

1 teaspoon baking powder

70 g fresh white breadcrumbs

170 g cumquats

candied cumquats

500 ml orange juice

440 g castor sugar

1 kg cumquats

To prepare the candied cumquats, bring the orange juice and castor sugar to a boil in a large non-reactive saucepan, stirring to dissolve the sugar. Add the cumquats and bring the pan back to a boil. Simmer until the syrup is thick and the cumquats have collapsed and appear slightly translucent. Store the cumquats in the syrup in the refrigerator or seal in airtight jars.

Have ready a deep pot with a trivet placed on the bottom. Grease a 1 litre pudding basin with a little melted butter, then sprinkle in some flour and shake out the excess. Butter and flour the underside of a doubled sheet of foil – this will cover the pudding.

To make the pudding, preheat the oven to 200°C. Roast the almonds on a baking tray for about 5 minutes, shaking the tray to prevent the nuts from burning. Allow to cool, then grind in a food processor. Cream 170 g softened unsalted butter, the castor sugar and the orange zest in an electric mixer until pale and thick, then beat in the eggs, slowly and one at a time. Sift 145 g unbleached plain flour and the salt, ground cassia and baking powder and incorporate into the mixture with the breadcrumbs and ground almonds. The mixture will be quite stiff. Chop the unpeeled cumquats roughly and remove all seeds, then fold the fruit through the mixture.

Spoon the mixture into the prepared pudding basin and smooth the top. Cover with the buttered foil lid and fold tightly around the basin to seal. Tie a piece of kitchen string around the rim. You can make a string handle to make it easier to lift the pudding in and out of the pot by looping the excess string from around the rim through one side of the basin over to the other side and tying it in place. Put the pudding into the waiting pot, then pour in cold water to come halfway up the sides of the basin. Simmer gently for 4 hours, topping up the water level as necessary.

Allow the pudding to cool slightly before turning it out onto a serving plate. Arrange the candied cumquats around the pudding, then pour their syrup over. Serve with double cream. To reheat a cold pudding, return it to the basin and simmer as before for 45 minutes. Serves 10

candied cumquats   If kept submerged in their syrup, these cumquats will keep for a month or so, refrigerated, so it's worth preparing a big batch when you have access to the fruit.

Almond and Cumquat Tart with Chocolate Glaze

As noted elsewhere, cooking is about osmosis – it's about ideas sparking other ideas. I believe strongly in crediting authors of recipes, but sometimes the origins of an idea can become unclear. For example, I know that the almond tart in Stephanie Alexander's *Menus for Food Lovers* sent me in this direction, but I can't remember where the influence for the glaze came from.

1 quantity Sour Cream Pastry
  (page 127)
Candied Cumquats (page 251)

almond and cumquat filling
265 g almonds
1 teaspoon ground cassia
1 tablespoon cumquat zest
40 ml brandy
125 ml syrup from the Candied
  Cumquats (page 251)
softened unsalted butter

chocolate glaze
175 g Haigh's bittersweet
  couverture chocolate
¼ cup cream
50 g unsalted butter
1½ tablespoons syrup from the
  Candied Cumquats (page 251)
1 tablespoon brandy

Make and chill the pastry as instructed. Roll out the chilled pastry until about 3 mm thick and line a loose-bottomed 22 cm flan tin with it. Chill the pastry case in the freezer for 20 minutes.

Meanwhile, preheat the oven to 200°C. Line the chilled pastry case with foil, then weight it with dried beans or pastry weights and blind bake it for 15 minutes. Remove the foil and beans and return the pastry case to the oven for a further 10 minutes to ensure the pastry is crisp. Set the pastry case aside to cool. Leave the oven on.

To make the filling, roast the almonds on a baking tray for about 5 minutes, shaking the tray to prevent the nuts from burning. Allow to cool, then grind in a food processor. Reduce the oven temperature to 175°C. Mix the ground almonds with the ground cassia and cumquat zest. Stir in the brandy, cumquat syrup and 120 g softened unsalted butter. Pat the almond mixture into the pastry case and dot with a little more butter. Bake the tart for 30 minutes, until golden. Allow to cool to room temperature.

To make the glaze, bring a saucepan of water to a boil. Roughly chop the couverture chocolate and put it into a mixing bowl with the remaining ingredients. Turn the heat off under the saucepan, but leave the pan in place. Stand the bowl over the pan and stir gently until the chocolate has melted and all the ingredients have combined. Allow to cool, then pour over the filling in the tart. Leave at room temperature to set. Serve with candied cumquats alongside. **Serves 10**

couverture chocolate   Don't be tempted to use anything other than couverture chocolate for the glaze on this wonderfully rich tart.

Fig and Walnut Tart

I made this tart so often at the Pheasant Farm that I became tired of it, and was almost embarrassed by the enthusiastic response as it couldn't be more simple. Twenty years later, I now enjoy making it again, having replaced the original cream with crème fraîche. Last time I made it, I topped the tart with slices of fresh lime and was transported. A recipe is only a base, after all.

180 g walnuts
330 g dried figs
6 free-range egg whites
250 g soft dark-brown sugar
crème fraîche
slices of candied *or* fresh lime
  (optional)

Preheat the oven to 220°C. Roast the walnuts on a baking tray for about 5 minutes, shaking the trays to prevent the nuts from burning. If they are not fresh season's, rub the walnuts in a clean tea towel to remove the bitter skins, then sieve away the skins. Allow to cool. Reduce the oven temperature to 180°C.

Line and grease a 24 cm springform cake tin. Remove the hard stem from each fig, then chop the figs into small pieces (this should give you 1½ cups). Toss the walnuts and fig pieces together.

In the bowl of an electric mixer, whisk the egg whites to soft peaks, then slowly add the soft dark-brown sugar in heaped tablespoons until incorporated and the resultant meringue is thick and stiff. Take a spoonful of the meringue and mix it through the figs and walnuts. Tip this back into the meringue and fold it through. Spoon the meringue mixture into the prepared cake tin and bake for 45–50 minutes; until the tart pulls away from the sides and feels 'set' on top.

Allow to cool and serve with a good dollop of crème fraîche. Candied or even fresh lime is a wonderful accompaniment to this tart – decorate the edge of the tart with a ring of fine, fine slices of the lime. The tart is meant to be sticky and soft and will be rustic in appearance, so don't fret if it falls apart as you serve it. **Serves 8**

summerautumnwinterspring

The Jinker Trip   I have to be honest and say that when I first moved to the Barossa, the Beer family shack at Port Parham came as a bit of a shock to me, the Sydneysider so used to the ocean. Beach to me meant crashing waves and white sand, and it took a long time to realise the special appeal of this beach on Gulf St Vincent.

For starters, there are the tides. At Port Parham it seems the sea pulls out forever, leaving acres of cold, wet sand to encounter before you can venture out for a swim (not a surf, mind you) and a shoreline rimmed with seaweed. After Sydney's rocky headlands and myriad coves and beaches, the flat, flat coastline seemed a little less exciting. Same with the seaside dwellings, many of them humble weekenders clad in corrugated iron or similar. 'Oh dear,' I thought, on my first encounter thirty years ago.

However, it took no time at all to appreciate the blue-swimmer crabs that are to be had here. My first memory of Port Parham crab is of sandwiches made by

Col's mum. She had prepared a treat for us to take on our first visit to the land we'd bought sight unseen before we came to make the Barossa our home – the land that was later sold to buy the block that became the Pheasant Farm. These were doorstopper sandwiches of good white bread from Algar's, the now-defunct bakery at Mallala, and they were thick with crabmeat. I've been hooked ever since.

While I struggled to come to grips with Port Parham, I could always be coerced into a weekend there when the crabs were running, but even then I couldn't ever quite 'get' the Beer excitement. Crabbing was definitely An Expedition, and not for the faint-hearted. The cupboards in the shack were full of old jumpers and sandshoes of every shape and size – as nice as walking on wet sand can be, a nipping crab can really hurt. And you had to be prepared for the cold: the best crabbing is done at night and the crabbers were often out for hours; the state of the tide dictating how far they had to walk before they found water. All this before they even started looking for, let alone catching, crabs! Once in the water, a tin baby's bath, with rakes trailing out of it, was tied to someone's waist and someone else again had to be responsible for the Tilley lamp, always a drama.

Let's just say that I never really caught the crabbing bug. Instead, I was the 'B' company, as Col's dad used to call it: 'Be there when they go and be there when they get back'. Anyway, someone had to stay with the girls, too young to be part of it all. But none of the above stopped me from joining in the finale: as soon as I heard the fire being lit under the old copper outside the shack, I'd be at the ready to help eat the catch.

The tradition of cooking the crabs hasn't altered for decades. One of the crab-bing party is responsible for bringing a bucket of sea water back in which to cook the catch, and the crabbers dry off and get rugged up while the water comes to a boil. A couple of dozen crabs at a time are flung into the copper and cooked for no more than three minutes, then they're scooped out to drain and cool a little on the old wire bed frame set aside for this purpose alone. Eating these glorious crabs as we stand around the fire, even in summer, has to rate as one of the great food experiences of my life.

And then came the jinker. Actually an old car frame made up so that it stands 1.8 metres above the ground, it has proved a boon for going crabbing and swimming with the minimum of fuss and the maximum of fun. Now the famous Parham tides don't bother me at all – we have the jinker to take us to the water! How I wish we'd had this contraption when our children were young, especially when I see our little grandchildren, Zöe, Max and Lily, all enjoying it. The jinker makes the water so accessible – and now I realise what I've missed while sitting on the sidelines. After all these years, I've finally 'got' the Port Parham bug.

The crabbing tub sits easily on the back of the jinker. The driver (most often Colin, with help from Max) and three passengers have seats on the top deck. But my favourite position is sitting on the edge, toes dangling, as we head out after water – and crabs.

Who needs a boat, and what could be better on a late spring evening, with the sun setting over the other side of the Gulf? The Sydney person I once was now loves this simple coastline – there is absolutely no artifice or pretence here. What you see is what you get, and I love it. I now know that this place can be as beautiful as the Greek Islands – but I've always known that the blue-swimmer crabs are better here than anywhere else in the world.

Strawberry Jam

When the very first of the strawberries appear I love to make jam. Strawberry jam is actually far more difficult to make and set than you'd think, however. The berries are low in pectin and best cooked as soon after picking as possible, without having been refrigerated, to preserve the pectin and the flavour. This jam was heavenly with scones and cream from the Kernichs' dairy (see pages 316–19).

1 kg ripe strawberries (I prefer
   the variety Chandler)
1 kg castor sugar

Wash and hull the strawberries. Cut the berries in half if they are large, then put them into a large non-reactive bowl and toss with the castor sugar until the sugar is evenly distributed. Cover and leave overnight to macerate.

The following day, transfer the strawberries and sugar to a large, wide non-reactive pot – it needs to be two-thirds deeper than the height of the strawberries as the jam froths violently during cooking. Bring rapidly to a boil and cook vigorously over the fiercest heat you can muster until the syrup has reduced – this should take no more than 20 minutes if you are to retain maximum fresh-ness of flavour and brightness of colour. Pour into sterilised, hot jars and seal well, then invert the jars to create a vacuum. **Makes 1.3 litres**

small batches   Strawberry jam should always be cooked in small batches, otherwise you lose the fresh flavour of the fruit. Choosing a wide pot will help, too, as the liquid will evaporate quickly and the fruit won't overcook.

pectin   If you have no option but to refrigerate your strawberries, add lemon juice just before cooking to boost the pectin and provide an edge.

Asparagus Soup

Some years ago I made asparagus soup for hundreds of concert-goers during the internationally acclaimed Barossa Music Festival. The festival is held in early October, so the asparagus was perfect. I was tempted to include that recipe here, but my editor gently chided me that a recipe for four would be of more use. What I can tell you is that the following can be multiplied successfully to feed a crowd.

40 asparagus spears

sea salt

1 large brown onion

¼ cup extra-virgin olive oil

350 ml light chicken stock

125 ml cream

freshly ground black pepper

1 tablespoon plucked chervil

Snap the woody ends off the asparagus – you should be left with about 400 g asparagus spears. Cook the spears in boiling salted water in a non-reactive saucepan until just tender.

Finely chop the onion, then sauté it in the olive oil until translucent. Purée the onion with the cooked asparagus in a food processor or blender, then pass through a coarse sieve and discard the solids. Gently warm the asparagus purée in a non-reactive saucepan with the stock and cream (this soup is very indulgent – if you want to stretch it a bit further just thin it with more stock). Season with salt and pepper and scatter on the chervil before serving. Serves 3–4

Potato Baked with Meyer Lemon

Spring is the time for new potatoes, so why relegate them to playing second fiddle? With great waxy potatoes to hand, I happily serve this flavour-driven dish for lunch, perhaps with a little cheese and a salad to follow. I now find it hard to believe that potatoes didn't appear on the menu at the Pheasant Farm for a decade simply because good varieties were hard to find. Thank goodness things change.

12 evenly sized waxy potatoes
 (kipflers are good)

1½ Meyer lemons (the half
 cut lengthwise)

¼ cup rosemary sprigs

¼ cup extra-virgin olive oil

3 teaspoons sea salt

freshly ground black pepper

Preheat the oven to 230°C. Cut the potatoes in half lengthwise and the whole lemon into eighths and the half into quarters, then spread these over a large, shallow baking dish, leaving space between the pieces. Scatter on the rosemary, then drizzle with the olive oil to coat, and season with the salt. Bake for 10 minutes, then turn the potato and lemon pieces and bake for a further 10 minutes until evenly browned. Season with a little more salt, if necessary, and some pepper and serve immediately. **Serves 4**

lemons   If Meyer lemons aren't in season, choose thin-skinned young fruit of another variety.

Silverbeet with Quark and Roasted Almonds

I love silverbeet from the vegetable garden – just-picked, the firm leaves and snapping stems are full of vigour and bursting with goodness. So often the stems are trimmed away and discarded, but these are more important in this dish than the leaves and provide flavour and texture. If it's possible in your State, have a go at making quark with unpasteurised milk to appreciate the extra dimension it gives.

80 g flaked almonds

1 tablespoon extra-virgin
 olive oil

8 stalks super-fresh silverbeet

20 g butter

⅓ cup fresh quark

sea salt

freshly ground black pepper

Preheat the oven to 200°C. Scatter the almonds over a small baking tray and drizzle with the olive oil, then bake until golden brown, about 5 minutes.

Wash and dry the silverbeet thoroughly. Cut out the stalks, then cut these into 3 cm lengths. Coarsely shred the greens. Put the stalks and greens into a deep saucepan with the butter, then cover with a lid and sauté for 3–5 minutes, until the stalks just start to soften. Toss with the roasted almonds and quark and season with salt and pepper and serve immediately. Serves 4

quark   Quark is a fresh curd cheese that varies in consistency and sourness depending on how long it is left to drain and whether the milk used is fresh or slightly sour, low or high in fat, raw or pasteurised. For the dish photographed opposite I used Richard Thomas's quark recipe that appears in Will Studd's book *Chalk and Cheese*. I used raw milk and wrapped the fresh cheese in muslin and hung it to drain for 24 hours. The cheese was rich and crumbly, but a good-quality commercial quark available from delis will also work well here.

Bread and Purslane Salad

When you're interested in food you never stop learning. I was sitting at a table at Marchetti's Latin in Melbourne listening to Greg Malouf, restaurateur and author of *Arabesque*, talking of bread and purslane salad, a childhood dish. Most cooks have the facility to 'taste' something they hear described or read about, and I was so fascinated I made it as soon as I got home. Thanks, Greg, I love it!

4 handfuls purslane

2 quarters preserved lemon

4 large anchovy fillets

3 thick door-stopper slices of
   wood-fired white bread

120 ml extra-virgin olive oil

1 clove garlic

2 tablespoons verjuice

sea salt

freshly ground black pepper

Preheat the oven to 220°C. Meanwhile, wash the purslane, then nip it into 3 cm lengths. Wash the preserved lemon, removing the pulp, and slice the rind into thin strips. Rip the anchovies into small pieces. Set aside.

Remove the crusts from the bread and brush both sides with half the olive oil. Toast on baking trays in the oven until golden brown, turning after the first side has coloured. Rub the toast with the cut garlic clove and rip into bite-sized pieces, then scatter these over the base of a wide, shallow dish. Sprinkle the toast with half the verjuice to moisten it. It is important that the bread is not soggy.

In a large mixing bowl, toss the toast with the purslane, preserved lemon and anchovy pieces. Whisk the remaining olive oil and verjuice together and season with salt and pepper. Serve the salad and dress just before eating. This rustic salad teams perfectly with fish or chicken. You could also add goat's cheese for a substantial luncheon dish for two. Serves 4

Raw Beetroot Salad with Orange Zest

At the risk of sounding like a broken record, you should try growing your own beetroot. Picking beetroot before they are overblown ensures a sweetness that's hard to find in the markets, where the vegetables might be older than is desirable. I believe the size of a beetroot dictates how it should be used, but often beetroot of varying sizes are sold together in a bunch, which leads to wastage.

1 bunch small beetroot

1 small orange

¼ cup flat-leaf parsley leaves

1 tablespoon lemon juice

⅓ cup fruity green extra-virgin
  olive oil

½ teaspoon sea salt

freshly ground black pepper

Wash and peel the beetroot, then grate them as finely as possible to yield 2 cups. The finer the beetroot, the more luscious the salad. Remove the zest from the orange with a potato peeler, being careful to avoid all pith, and cut it into fine strips. Toss the grated beetroot with the orange zest and the parsley. Whisk the lemon juice and olive oil together and dress the salad, then season with salt and pepper. **Serves 4**

bitter orange   This salad is given another twist if you make it with a bitter orange.

Fresh Goat's Curd with Walnut Oil, Rocket and Walnut Bread

I first tasted really great walnut oil in a tiny shop in a Parisian back street with Stephanie Alexander. Accompanying our tasting of this amazingly vibrant oil was a dish of goat's curd and tiny croutons. The juxtaposition of these simple flavours really impacted on me. Search out the best imported walnut oils, but buy them in the smallest quantity available as rancidity is a problem.

100 g walnuts

sea salt

1 Walnut Bread baguette
  (page 322)

walnut oil

4 small handfuls rocket leaves

freshly ground black pepper

340 g fresh goat's curd

Preheat the oven to 220°C. Roast the walnuts on a baking tray for about 5 minutes, shaking the tray to prevent the nuts from burning. If they are not fresh season's, rub the walnuts in a clean tea towel to remove the bitter skins, then transfer to a coarse sieve and shake to remove the skin. Toss the walnuts with a little salt.

Slice the baguette into 1.5 cm thick pieces and brush both sides with walnut oil (you'll need ⅓ cup). Toast on baking trays in the oven until golden brown, then turn to toast the other side.

To assemble the salad, wash and dry the rocket leaves, then toss with the walnuts and a little pepper. Divide the goat's curd between 4 entrée plates, then make an indentation in the middle of the curd with the back of a spoon. Pour 1 tablespoon walnut oil into this little well. Arrange the rocket and walnuts around the curd, put the toasted walnut bread to the side and serve immediately. The idea is that as you dip and eat, the walnut oil becomes integrated with the goat's cheese. Just delicious. **Serves 4**

walnut oil   The quality of the walnut oil is integral to this dish. The best oils may be too strong – if this is the case, dilute the oil with a flavourless oil such as grapeseed. Also, walnut oil does not have a long shelf-life and is particularly prone to rancidity, so check the state of yours carefully. Walnut oil is best stored in the refrigerator and used soon after opening.

Green Bean Salad with Seared Tuna, Pullet Eggs and Wild Olives

I hesitate calling this a Niçoise salad, but that is, of course, its base. The first beans of late spring always make me want to serve this – while keeping their colour is vital, so is making sure they are cooked. In contrast, the tuna should be quite raw in the middle. I couldn't help adding wild olives to the dish being photographed as the trees are such a part of the Barossa – consider them optional.

400 g green beans

sea salt

4 pullet eggs

1 small handful basil leaves

1 punnet cherry tomatoes

4 × 150 g thick tuna steaks

5 tablespoons extra-virgin
  olive oil

1 tablespoon red-wine vinegar

freshly ground black pepper

Top and tail the beans, then cut them in half. Blanch the beans in boiling salted water until tender, then drain well. Set aside. Cook the eggs in simmering salted water for 4 minutes, then drop into cold water to inhibit cooking (they should be soft-boiled).

Shred the basil leaves finely and cut each cherry tomato in half crosswise. Keep a little basil aside, then toss the beans with the remaining basil and the tomatoes and divide between 4 plates.

Drizzle the tuna steaks with 1 tablespoon of the olive oil and heat a non-stick frying pan until very hot. Sear the tuna for 2 minutes on the first side, then season and turn and cook for 1 minute only. The steaks will be rare in the middle. Allow to rest for 5 minutes, then cut into chunks and toss with the remaining basil.

Whisk the remaining olive oil with the vinegar, then season with salt and pepper. Gently toss the tuna chunks with the bean salad, then cut the soft-boiled eggs in half and add to the top, and drizzle over the vinaigrette. Serve with salt and pepper on the table. Serves 4

The Beehive

Of the many unique things in the Barossa Valley, Mark and Gloria Rosenzweig's stationary Berlepsch-Dzierzon beehive is certainly one. Originally from Silesia, along with many of our early settlers, this hive has been in use for more than a century without alteration.

The individual hives are kept in a long, very narrow, L-shaped corrugated-iron shed, closed to the weather on one side. Boxes stand on planks suspended from beams by metal rods, each of which passes through a pot of sump oil to keep ants at bay. These boxes are quite different from the hives that open up from the top that you see stacked around the countryside. Instead, each has a glass window through which any activity can be checked. A door on the side gives access to the frames that carry the honeycomb, and the front has a landing platform for the bees.

Most beekeepers live a roving life, moving their bees from blossom to blossom, but these bees rely entirely on the nearby gums. Transient hives have been left too close occasionally, which can be disastrous for the Rosenzweigs' bees – they can starve if their usual blossom source is stripped before they get to it, such is the limit of their range.

I'm not at all frightened by bees, and for years I had a friend who left his hives on our property. Nonetheless, I wondered whether I would feel quite the same after donning a beekeeper's outfit to see the honey collection at close quarters. Mark is in fact allergic to bees, which seems unfair for a third-generation apiarist, but I felt confident he knew exactly what he was doing – after all, he takes danger in his stride each time he collects the honey.

Kitted up in a white boiler suit, gloves and a helmet with a scarf, I set out after Mark. The bees that day were crowded on their inspection window, not moving off of their own accord, so Mark quietened them down with a portable smoker. He carefully slid out the first of the honeycomb frames, brushing off the bees in the process, and put it, already oozing, into a bucket before moving further into the hive. Finally he came to the frame with the eggs; this he left in place, and then carefully shut the hive.

Gloria's tiny collection room was heady with the scent of honey and smoke as she puffed the smoker to subdue the few bees inside. Every implement used seems as old as the hives themselves: a turkey feather to brush the groggy bees away from the frame, and a hand-forged knife with a curved blade warmed over a flame to slice off the wax capping the cells. The afternoon light streamed through the small windows, dazzling us as it played against the gold of the honey frame.

Gloria loaded the first frame into the extractor – an ornate and very old steel drum – and as she turned the handle the honey ran into the bottom. This fresh honey was viscous and full of flavour – I have never tasted better. Honey from this hive has a consistency of flavour that wild honey lacks, the only real change occurring when the seasons get confused and the red gums blossom at the same time as the blue gums.

Best of all is the thick, treacly, almost black honey extracted from the wax capping on the frames. This is kept especially for those traditional cooks, often of an advanced age these days, who feel it makes the best honigkuchen, a strong Christmas custom here. How I love that wonderful Barossa ethos of wasting nothing – it throws up the most wonderful surprises you would never come across otherwise.

I keep thinking of that expression 'the bee's knees', and that's what honey is when it's straight from the source. You'll never get better.

Sorrel Tart

This is a sentimental favourite. At my first-ever meal at Claude's in Sydney, then owned by Damien Pignolet, a sorrel tart preceded an amazing bouillabaise cooked for the whole restaurant. With my love of things sour, it was an instant hit with me. Damien's skill and his pâté brisée are legendary, but I've taken the easier option here and use my foolproof sour cream pastry.

1 quantity Sour Cream Pastry
   (page 127)
1 onion
300 g sorrel
50 g butter
4 × 61 g free-range eggs
125 ml cream
½ teaspoon sea salt
½ teaspoon freshly ground
   black pepper
crème fraîche

Make and chill the pastry as instructed. Line a 22 cm loose-bottomed flan tin with the pastry, then refrigerate it for 20 minutes. Meanwhile, preheat the oven to 200°C.

Line the chilled pastry case with foil, then weight it with dried beans or pastry weights and blind bake for 15 minutes. Remove the foil and beans and return the pastry case to the oven for a further 10 minutes to ensure the pastry is crisp. Set the pastry case aside to cool a little. Reduce the oven temperature to 180°C.

Finely chop the onion and remove the stems from the sorrel if it is anything other than very young. Sauté the onion in the butter in a frying pan until soft and translucent. Add the sorrel and toss over a gentle heat until it has wilted. Remove the pan from the heat and purée the sorrel mixture in a food processor.

Lightly whisk the eggs with the cream, salt and pepper, then whisk in the sorrel purée. Pour the mixture into the pastry case and bake for 35–40 minutes until just set. Allow to cool a little before cutting and serving with a generous dollop of crème fraîche. **Serves 8**

sorrel   In spring, when the sorrel is young, you can include the stalks, as they will not be fibrous. In fact, the whole leaf is so tender when young that it almost melts when cooked, intensifying the piquancy that's so delicious in this dish.

Artichoke, Pea and Pancetta Risotto

I have two people very close to me who don't really cook but who like to make risotto: Colin is one, the other is Clare Bogan, who keeps me in touch with what I should be making in the Export Kitchen for people like her. Although I can hear Clare saying, 'Can I leave out the artichokes? They're too hard to peel!', the following really is a dish for everyone.

18 thin slices pancetta

6 artichokes

250 ml verjuice

1 litre golden chicken stock

2 large brown onions

3 cloves garlic

160 g butter

¼ cup extra-virgin olive oil

1 × 50 g packet dried
  Surprise peas

750 g arborio rice

¾ cup roughly chopped
  flat-leaf parsley

2 cups freshly shaved
  Parmigiano-Reggiano

sea salt

freshly ground black pepper

Preheat the oven to 200°C. Crisp the pancetta on baking trays for about 5 minutes. Set aside. Prepare each artichoke by pulling away the outside leaves to reveal the heart. Using a paring knife, trim around the base of the heart and cut off the stalk. Cut away the fibrous choke and immerse the artichoke in the verjuice to stop oxidisation.

Bring the stock to a boil in a non-reactive saucepan, then reduce to a simmer. Finely chop the onions and garlic. Melt 100 g of the butter in a heavy-based, non-reactive pot and add the olive oil to inhibit burning. Gently sauté the onion and garlic in the butter and oil until almost translucent. Remove the artichokes from the verjuice, reserving the verjuice. Add the artichoke hearts and dried peas to the pan and sauté gently. Turn up the heat and add the rice, stirring well until it is gleaming, and sauté for another 3 minutes. Strain the verjuice, then add it to the rice and let it bubble away.

Reduce the heat to medium and add the first ladleful of stock, stirring to incorporate it. Continue cooking, adding a ladleful of stock as the last is absorbed and stirring all the while. The rice will take about 20 minutes to cook and shouldn't go beyond being al dente.

Crumble the pancetta, then fold it through the risotto with the remaining butter and the parsley. Check for seasoning and serve with the freshly shaved Parmigiano and a grinding of pepper. Serves 6

surprise peas   Truly fresh peas are the ultimate in this dish, but they are difficult to find unless you grow them in your own garden. When I heard that an Italian friend uses dried Surprise peas when making risotto, I had to give it a try, so amazed was I at the thought. Lo and behold, they retained their colour and shape much better than fresh peas, and their flavour permeated the rice beautifully.

Ravioli of Pea, Asparagus and Chervil

As our mood lightens with spring weather, so does our food. This is the time to capture the freshness of new season's asparagus and peas, and this dish is the perfect vehicle, the chervil adding a delicate but important note. The great thing about handmade ravioli is that you dictate the size of the parcel – it can be anything from a large one per person to lots of tiny ones.

1 quantity Duck Egg Pasta
  (page 40)
sea salt
2 kg just-picked peas
  in their pods
8 asparagus spears
1¼ cups loosely packed
  chervil leaves
freshly ground black pepper
1 free-range egg white
20 g butter
1 tablespoon extra-virgin
  olive oil
1 tablespoon lemon juice

Make and chill the pasta dough as instructed.

Bring a saucepan of salted water to a boil. Shell the fresh peas. Snap the woody ends off the asparagus spears and discard, then roughly chop the tops. Put the peas and asparagus into the water and allow to return to a boil. Turn the pan down to a simmer and cook gently until the peas and asparagus are tender but still retain their colour. Drain well.

Roughly chop 1 cup of the chervil, then mash this with the peas and asparagus and season well with salt and pepper.

Cut the chilled pasta dough into 2 pieces. Using a pasta machine, roll each piece of dough through the settings until you reach the finest. It is important when rolling this pasta dough for ravioli that you continue rolling to ensure it is as fine as possible. Trim the ends of the pasta sheets to square them up, ensuring the sheets are the same length. Remove any excess flour from the pasta and brush the sheets with egg white that has been lightly whipped with a fork. Place ½ teaspoon of filling at 3 cm intervals minimum down a pasta sheet, then position another sheet on top, gently pushing down between the mounds of filling to seal the parcels and to get rid of any air bubbles. Cut the sheets into square 'pillows' using a knife, or use a round 6–8 cm pastry cutter.

Bring a pot of salted water to a boil. Plunge the ravioli into the water, then allow the pan to return to a boil and simmer for 3 minutes. Drain well.

Heat the butter and olive oil in a frying pan until nut-brown and foaming, then add the cooked ravioli and toss gently. Add the remaining chervil and the lemon juice and season with pepper. Serve immediately. **Serves 4**

fresh peas   As the sugar in peas turns to starch very quickly after picking, the peas used in this dish need to be just picked, otherwise they will take a lot of cooking (in fact, if I don't have super-fresh peas, I prefer to use frozen ones in this recipe). If you are using older peas, you will need to cook them until they're grey–green and soft enough to purée. The asparagus will need less cooking.

Pasta Rags with Goat's Curd, Zucchini Flowers and Green Almonds

This is a truly sexy dish. It's all about the silky texture of the handmade pasta, the creaminess of the melting cheese, the vibrancy of the zucchini flowers, the freshness of the lemon juice and the crunch of the green almonds.

1 small quorm pink garlic

extra-virgin olive oil

1 quantity Fresh Pasta

  (page 122)

8 × 8 cm zucchini with flowers

  attached

25 g butter

40 green almonds

100 g fresh goat's curd

3 teaspoons lemon juice

1 cup flat-leaf parsley leaves

sea salt

freshly ground black pepper

Preheat the oven to 180°C. Brush the garlic quorm with 1 tablespoon olive oil and roast in the smallest ovenproof dish you have for 45 minutes until golden brown and caramelised. Allow to cool a little, then squeeze the roasted cloves from their skins and set aside.

Make, chill and roll the pastry as instructed, then cut it into 'rags' and spread out on clean tea towels until required (this prevents the pasta rags from sticking together or drying out too fast).

Blanch the zucchini and their flowers in a little simmering water with 2 teaspoons of the butter for 3 minutes or until just tender. Rest for 5 minutes before slicing in half lengthwise, flowers included. Peel the husks from the green almonds and discard.

Heat the remaining butter in a frying pan until nut-brown, then sauté the sliced zucchini and their flowers and the green almonds for 3–4 minutes. Bring a large pot of salted water to a boil and cook the pasta rags for 2 minutes (alternatively, cook the pasta in advance and reheat it gently in the microwave). Drain thoroughly and transfer to a warmed serving dish. Add the zucchini, caramelised garlic, green almonds, goat's curd, lemon juice and parsley and toss. The goat's curd will melt beautifully with the heat of the pasta. Season with salt and pepper and serve immediately. This dish is great served cold, too. **Serves 4**

green almonds   If you don't have access to green almonds, you can also use ½ cup slivered almonds – brush these with 1 tablespoon extra-virgin olive oil and roast at 200°C until golden.

Spaghettini with Sardines, Sultanas and Breadcrumbs

Even before my first visit to Sicily in 1999, I had a voracious appetite when it came to reading about that island's food. It was a privilege, then, to be invited by the International Olive Oil Council to visit during the olive crush. This simple but sublime dish is an example of the traditional fare we enjoyed, given here with sultanas rather than currants, a suggestion of our photographer, Simon Griffiths.

½ cup sultanas

125 ml verjuice

12 fresh sardines

¾ cup flaked almonds

extra-virgin olive oil

2 cups breadcrumbs (from
 stale wood-fired bread)

1 large brown onion

8 anchovy fillets

200 g best-quality dried
 spaghettini

unsalted butter

2 tablespoons roughly chopped
 wild fennel *or* flat-leaf parsley

2 tablespoons lemon juice

sea salt

freshly ground black pepper

lemon wedges

Put the sultanas and verjuice in a bowl and soak for 1 hour, or microwave on high for 2 minutes. Drain.

Scale the sardines, then cut off the heads. Slit the underbelly of each sardine and remove the entrails. Using your thumb and index finger, hold a sardine down at the point where the head meets the backbone. With your other hand, pull the head backwards, taking the backbone and tail as you go. This will leave you with a boned and butterflied sardine. Repeat with the remaining sardines, then flatten out the fillets. Rinse well under cold water, pat dry with kitchen paper and set aside.

Preheat the oven to 200°C. Rub the almonds with 1 tablespoon olive oil and toast in the oven until golden brown. Rub the breadcrumbs with 2 tablespoons olive oil, then scatter on a baking tray and toast in the oven until golden brown.

Roughly chop the onion and anchovies separately. Sauté the onion in ¼ cup olive oil in a frying pan until translucent. Stir in the toasted almonds, drained sultanas and chopped anchovy, then set aside.

Bring a large pot of salted water to a boil and cook the spaghettini until al dente according to the manufacturer's instructions. Drain.

Meanwhile, heat a knob of butter with a splash of olive oil and pan-fry the sardine fillets over medium heat for 2 minutes on the first side and 1 minute on the second, then add the chopped fennel or parsley and set aside.

Toss the onion mixture, breadcrumbs and lemon juice through the cooked spaghettini and season with salt and pepper. Gently toss the sardines and fennel through the pasta and serve immediately with lemon wedges alongside. Serves 4

Port Parham Crabs

Eating crabs at Col's family shack at the very tidal Port Parham on the Gulf St Vincent is one of our favourite traditions, as I describe on pages 263–4. The flavour of just-caught and cooked crabs is a world apart from crabs offered commercially – there's nothing better than rolling up the sleeves and demolishing one after the other with little more than a glass of our semillon or a beer.

sea water *or* salted water

live blue-swimmer crabs

Bring a good quantity of sea water to a boil in a large, deep pot and toss in several of the crabs without crowding the pot. Boil for 3 minutes only, then drain and set the crabs aside to cool a little (turn them onto their backs to retain the delicious juices). Allow the pot to return to the boil and continue the process until all the crabs are cooked. They are at their very best when eaten warm.

Crab Cakes

Port Parham has always been about the Beer family gathering together and Col's late mum cooking huge breakfasts for everyone, most often in the electric frying pan. This pan is symbolic of shack culture and is the perfect size for cooking all these crab cakes at once, as you can see in the pictures opposite.

1 × 2.5 cm piece ginger

4 spring onions

250 g just-cooked blue-
   swimmer crabmeat

½ cup fresh breadcrumbs

½ cup firmly packed
   coriander leaves

¼ cup finely shredded basil

extra-virgin olive oil

sea salt

freshly ground black pepper

1 tablespoon lemon juice

unbleached plain flour

Peel and grate the ginger, then finely chop the spring onions. Mix these with the crabmeat, bread-crumbs, herbs and 1 tablespoon olive oil, then add 2 teaspoons salt, 8 grinds of pepper and the lemon juice to taste. Form the mixture into small balls, then flatten these into discs.

Season a little flour with salt and pepper, then lightly coat each crab cake with this. Heat olive oil in a frying pan and shallow-fry the crab cakes until golden brown, then turn and cook the other side. Drain the crab cakes on crumpled kitchen paper while frying the next batch. Serve with Crab-mustard Mayonnaise (page 294) or lemon wedges. **Makes 6**

crabmeat   When making these crab cakes, I use crabmeat that is only just cooked as it is still a little gelatinous and survives being cooked again.

Crab-mustard Mayonnaise

When Stephanie Alexander visited us while researching material for *Stephanie's Australia* we took her to Port Parham for a feast of crabs and she immediately made her mark by adding the mustard of the crab to the mayonnaise we made. I've done the same ever since. This is the perfect way to introduce crab mustard (almost my favourite part) to the more tentative eater.

2 free-range egg yolks
¼ cup crab mustard
juice of 1 lemon
375 ml good-quality
    extra-virgin olive oil
sea salt
freshly ground black pepper

Blend the egg yolks, crab mustard and half the lemon juice in a food processor. You can continue in the food processor, but for the very best mayonnaise, transfer the egg mixture to a bowl and use a whisk. Start by adding the oil drop by drop and then in a slow but steady stream, until the mixture is thick and glossy (for more about making mayonnaise, turn to page 20). Season with salt and pepper and add more lemon juice if it is needed.

crab mustard   Crab liver is yellowy-orange in colour, which no doubt is the reason it is known as the 'mustard' (in some parts of the world it is also known as the tomally). It is found inside the shell and is sadly discarded by most. It provides a rich flavour and can simply be added to the meat of the crab however you plan to eat it.

Mustard-bread Crab Sandwiches

When I was searching for a dish that replicated the simple way we eat at Port Parham, I thought of a crab risotto, omelette or salad. But the flavour of the blue-swimmer crab is such a perfect one in itself that I decided the best option was to follow the KISS principle. So here's a sandwich! The moistness of the bread, made with conventional mustard, works beautifully with the crab.

2 thick slices *or* 1 tiny loaf
    Mustard Bread (page 323)
Crab-mustard Mayonnaise
    (see above)
80 g freshly picked blue-
    swimmer crabmeat
rocket *or* cress (optional)
lemon wedges (optional)
chilli jam (optional)

Slice the mustard bread in half lengthwise, then spread the mayonnaise on one half and the crabmeat on the other (check for any shell fragments first).

Serve with peppery greens, lemon wedges and chilli jam alongside so that the lucky recipient can choose the accompaniments. Makes 1

Flathead in Beer Batter

It always seemed so right for Flo Beer, my late mother-in-law, to make beer batter. When I first tasted hers I was astounded by its lightness – it's only recently I've learnt the difference preparing it 24 hours in advance makes (although I gather most fishermen know this trick). While the extra-virgin oil is my addition to this recipe, draining the fried fish on stale bread is a trick of Flo's.

6 flathead fillets

extra-virgin olive oil

slices of stale bread (optional)

sea salt

freshly ground black pepper

10 lemon wedges

beer batter

250 g self-raising flour

125 ml light beer

250 ml cold water

To make the batter, whisk the ingredients until smooth. Cover and refrigerate overnight or for a minimum of 1 hour – 24 hours is best of all, however.

When you are ready to cook, remove the skin from the flathead, if present. Pour olive oil into a shallow, heavy-based frying pan, leaving enough room to add the fish without spilling the oil, and heat until very hot. Dip the flathead fillets into the beer batter to coat, then gently lower them into the hot oil – you will need to do this in batches. Fry until crisp and golden brown on one side, then turn to cook the other. Transfer the cooked fish to a plate covered with slices of stale bread (or crumpled kitchen paper) to drain while you cook the next batch.

Serve the battered flathead with salt, pepper and lemon wedges. Serves 6

frying with extra-virgin olive oil   Extra-virgin olive oil is the healthiest and most delicious (albeit expensive) medium for deep-frying; it allows for minimal absorption and also gives you the crispest result. Choosing the right pan will enable you to shallow-fry rather than deep-fry, and thereby use less oil. The flavour of the oil diminishes at high temperatures, so you won't want to use it for a salad afterwards, but if filtered you can reuse it several times when cooking.

Sashimi of Whiting

This can easily be made with any firm, white-fleshed fish – snapper, gar, coral trout and flathead work well – or salmon or ocean trout. But unless you've caught it yourself or have access to a supplier like John Sussman, a former South Australian who provides amazingly fresh fish (such as the beautiful specimen opposite) to restaurants and the general public, then try another dish.

2 small shallots

125 ml verjuice

2 tablespoons freshly plucked
 chervil

¼ cup extra-virgin olive oil

sea salt

freshly ground black pepper

2 fillets super-fresh whiting

lemon wedges

Peel and chop the shallots, then put them into a non-reactive saucepan with the verjuice. Bring to a boil and cook until reduced by half. Mix this reduction with the chervil and olive oil and season with salt and pepper.

Remove the skin from the whiting, if present, then put the fillets into a deep glass dish and pour over the dressing. Leave to marinate for 30 minutes. Slice and serve with lemon wedges as an entrée or pre-dinner snack. Serves 4–6

Steamed Marron with Coriander and Lemon

Now that marron, the larger cousin of the yabby, are being farmed commercially, as my friend John Melbourne does on Kangaroo Island, they are available from early spring through to the end of autumn. Once you've mastered this simple way of cooking them, try blanching and then roasting or barbecuing them, anointed with butter or a good oil.

2 large live marron

¼ cup extra-virgin olive oil

1 cup coriander leaves

sea salt

freshly ground black pepper

1 lemon

Stun the marron by putting them into the freezer in a tightly covered container for 30 minutes. Using a large and very sharp knife, cut each marron in half lengthwise firmly and quickly. Brush with the extra-virgin olive oil and scatter with half the coriander.

Bring a large pot of water to a boil and place a steamer on top – this will work best if you have a wok burner. Put the marron halves into the steamer, then cover it tightly and rapidly return the pot to a boil. Steam for 10–13 minutes, depending on the size of the marron. Drain.

Arrange the marron on a large serving platter, then season with salt and pepper and scatter over the remaining coriander. Slice the lemon and serve alongside. Serves 4

coriander butter   Another way of presenting this dish is to blend half the coriander with 100 g softened unsalted butter and some salt and pepper – dollop this onto the just-cooked marron. Made to be eaten with the fingers!

Steamed Yabbies with Roasted Tomatoes, Lemon, Purslane and Basil

It was such a joy to get good spring rains in 2000 – for the first time in three years the dams on our home block filled. Our yabby dam has long been the centre of much of our spring and summer entertaining, and we had been lost without it and its inhabitants. This dish celebrates the return of the yabbies – the roasted tomato juice marries beautifully with the delicate meat.

24 large live yabbies

2 lemons

2 small handfuls purslane

2 small handfuls basil leaves

1½ tablespoons lemon juice

¼ cup extra-virgin olive oil

sea salt

freshly ground black pepper

roasted tomatoes

540 g Roma tomatoes

¼ cup extra-virgin olive oil

2 pinches castor sugar

sea salt

freshly ground black pepper

To prepare the tomatoes, preheat the oven to 220°C. Slice the tomatoes thickly and spread out on baking trays. Brush with the olive oil, then sprinkle with the castor sugar and season with salt and pepper. Roast for 40 minutes or until evenly cooked.

Meanwhile, stun the yabbies by putting them into the freezer in a tightly covered container for 20 minutes. Bring a large pot of water to a boil and place a steamer on top – this will work best if you have a wok burner. Remove the zest from the lemons in wide strips with a potato peeler. Put some of the stunned yabbies into the steamer with the zest, then cover tightly and rapidly return to a boil. Cook the yabbies for 4–6 minutes, depending on their size and the ferocity of the fire. (You will need to do this in batches.) Drain, then reserve 4 whole yabbies and the lemon zest. Peel the remaining yabbies and remove their intestinal tracts.

Pluck the purslane into 2 cm lengths, and shred the basil. Mix the peeled yabbies in a large bowl with the purslane, basil, lemon zest and roasted tomatoes. Whisk the lemon juice and olive oil together and season with salt and pepper, then toss this through the salad. Divide between individual plates or serve on a large platter, with the whole yabbies perched on top. **Serves 4**

purslane   If you can't get hold of purslane, which is salty and juicy, you can substitute lamb's lettuce, but you may need to add more salt.

Chicken Poached in Muslin

This is the dish to cook when you want to impress, but only consider it if you have a really good chicken (chook, really – it's hard to call a large bird by such a diminutive name). While I suggest a 2.5 kg bird here, the one photographed was actually 4 kg – a whopper, and so flavoursome.

1 × 2.5 kg free-range chicken
500 ml verjuice
2 litres golden chicken stock

stuffing

100 g chicken livers
125 ml extra-virgin olive oil
1 small onion
80 g speck *or* double-smoked
  bacon
1 cup fresh white breadcrumbs
1 teaspoon freshly chopped
  lemon thyme
1½ teaspoons freshly chopped
  marjoram
sea salt
freshly ground black pepper

To make the stuffing, trim the chicken livers, then pan-fry them in half the olive oil until still pink inside. Rest for 10 minutes, then cut into 1 cm dice. Finely chop the onion and speck. Sauté the onion in the remaining olive oil in the same pan until translucent. Combine the stuffing ingredients thoroughly in a bowl.

Stuff the cavity of the chicken, then truss the bird tightly. Wrap in a doubled layer of muslin, then twist the ends and tie them with kitchen string. The chicken will look like a large bonbon! Put it into a heavy-based pot – it must fit snugly but there must also be a little room around the edges. Combine the verjuice and stock and pour this over the chicken to cover it (you may have some left over, depending on the size of your pot; on the other hand, if you need more, add 1 part verjuice to 4 parts stock). Cover the pot with a lid and bring to a boil, then reduce to a slow simmer with the lid slightly ajar, using a simmer pad if necessary. Cook for 1½ hours, making sure the pot doesn't go beyond a slow simmer.

Remove the chicken, then wrap it well in plastic film and rest breast down for at least 30 minutes (don't worry, the bird will retain its heat during this resting period). Meanwhile, pour the cooking liquor into a tall jar and chill – the fat will float to the surface. Just before serving, scoop off the fat and discard it, then reheat enough cooking liquor to serve with the bird as a jus. Refrigerate the remaining cooking liquor to serve with leftovers the following day – it will jelly beautifully.

To serve, remove the plastic film and transfer the chicken to a platter (I decorate mine with fresh grapes and vine leaves). Unveil the chicken just before eating, then carve at the table and serve with the warmed juices. Serves 4

trials and tribulations   When cooking this once I rested the bird, still in its muslin jacket, breast up in a colander. The muslin stuck to the skin and dried out. Disaster! The above way is less fraught, or you could also unwrap the warm chicken very carefully and then rest it breast down.

cold chook   While I usually serve this chicken hot, it is delicious cold the next day, served with the jellied cooking liquor alongside – spoon the jellied stock onto the serving platter, as shown opposite, or dice it for extra effect.

Five-spice Barbecued Duck with Pickled Cherries

This dish came about one lazy Sunday afternoon when we had the family around for a late lunch/early dinner. Saskia had some ducks left over, so quickly whipped off the breasts and legs from the carcasses and massaged the meat with five-spice. Nothing could have been more simple, and the fatty skin of the Peking duck 'basted' the meat as it grilled.

2 × 1.2 kg Peking ducks
2½ teaspoons Chinese
  five-spice powder
Pickled Cherries (page 16)

Cut the legs and thighs away from each duck in one piece, then cut away each breast. Cut the drumsticks away from the thighs and remove the thigh bones. Freeze the drumsticks for another dish. Sprinkle the duck with the Chinese five-spice powder and rub it in well.

Preheat the barbecue to high – if you are using a wood-fired grill, make sure the fire has burnt down to glowing embers, then remove some of the red-hot coals. The idea is to seal the duck over a high heat without burning the skin and then finish cooking the meat over a more mellow heat. Seal the breasts and thigh meat quickly on the open grill side, rotating the pieces to achieve a crisscross pattern on the skin. Transfer the duck to the coolest corner of the barbecue plate and cook the thigh meat for 15 minutes on each side. As the breasts only need 6–7 minutes a side, add them to the hot plate when you turn the thigh meat (after 6–7 minutes a side the breast meat will still be pink – you can cook them for a longer time, if you prefer). Remove the duck from the heat and rest in a warm spot for 8 minutes. Serve with the pickled sour cherries and a bitter green salad. **Serves 4**

peking ducks   This dish will not be successful unless Peking ducks are used, as other breeds will not have enough fat for the cooking method used here.

Barley-stuffed Quail Baked in Vine Leaves

I love the way our vines let us know spring is on the way. The velvety-soft buds appear on the bare, gnarled vines, and before long the first leaves burst into yellowy-green brilliance. I celebrate the transformation of the vineyard by using the leaves to wrap quail, among other things. Quail just have to be eaten with the fingers to be fully enjoyed – real quail lovers suck the bones!

30 g butter

8 large free-range quail

16 young vine leaves

extra-virgin olive oil

3 lemons

barley stuffing

1 cup pearl barley

600–800 ml golden
  chicken stock

1 large brown onion

15 g butter

1 tablespoon currants

1 pinch salt

1 tablespoon lemon thyme
  leaves

freshly ground black pepper

To make the stuffing, soak the barley in water overnight. Next day, bring the chicken stock to a simmer in a saucepan. Drain the barley and finely chop the onion (you need ¾ cup chopped onion). Melt the butter in another saucepan and sauté the onion until translucent, then add the barley and sauté for 2 minutes. Stir in the currants and salt. Gradually add the hot stock to the barley a ladleful at a time, stirring until the liquid has been absorbed before adding more, as you do when making a risotto. Stir in the lemon thyme, then check the seasoning. Leave the stuffing to cool once the barley is cooked.

Heat the 30 g butter in a frying pan until nut-brown and foamy. Gently seal the quail in batches until golden brown, then remove, reserving the pan juices. Allow the quail to cool a little before filling with the barley stuffing. Brush the vine leaves with a little olive oil, then wrap each bird in 2 leaves, folding one over the breast and another over the back. Secure with toothpicks.

Preheat the oven to 220°C. Put the quail into a baking dish and drizzle with the reserved pan juices. Bake for 8–10 minutes, depending on the size of the quail. Allow to rest for 8 minutes. Slice the lemons, then serve the quail on a platter with the lemon alongside. **Serves 4**

Rabbit, Prune and Pancetta Pies

There is a particularly delightful freshness about these pies that could translate to any season, even summer. A real favourite, and a perfect way of using the legs of the rabbit. The cooking times given are for farmed rabbits and need to be adjusted if wild rabbits are to be used (these have wonderful flavour but are devoid of fat, so are very tricky cooking).

2 lemons

10 pitted prunes

2 × 1.4 kg farmed rabbits

¼ cup extra-virgin olive oil

2 tablespoons fresh thyme
  leaves

1 tablespoon freshly chopped
  sage

freshly ground black pepper

unsalted butter

3 slices pancetta

2 large brown onions

¼ cup verjuice

250 ml very reduced golden
  chicken stock

1 tablespoon freshly chopped
  flat-leaf parsley

1 heaped teaspoon unbleached
  plain flour

1 quantity Sour Cream Pastry
  (page 127)

1 free-range egg

1 tablespoon milk

Zest and juice the lemons. Put the prunes and lemon juice in a bowl with half the lemon zest and soak them overnight, or microwave on high for 2 minutes. Chop each reconstituted prune into 4 pieces. Cut the front and back legs away from the rabbits and remove the kidneys and livers from the saddles. Set the saddles aside for another dish. Put the rabbit legs, kidneys and livers into a flat glass dish with the remaining lemon zest and the olive oil, thyme, sage and ¼ teaspoon pepper. Toss and leave to marinate for a minimum of 1 hour.

Melt 30 g butter in a deep, heavy-based frying pan and gently seal the roughly chopped kidneys and livers, then remove and set aside. Seal the rabbit pieces in the same pan, then remove from the pan and set aside. Roughly chop the pancetta and cut each onion into sixths, then add these to the pan and cook until caramelised. Return the rabbit to the pan and deglaze it with the verjuice. Turn the heat down, then stand the pan on a simmer pad and simmer very gently for 20 minutes, with the lid slightly ajar. Remove the pan from the heat and set aside to rest for 30 minutes.

Take the meat off the bones and cut it into 1.5 cm dice, then combine with the kidney and liver (this should make about 3½ cups). Toss with the ingredients in the pan over a gentle heat. Add the prunes and lemon juice, the reduced stock and the parsley, then season with salt and pepper – the gentle heating of all the ingredients combines the flavours beautifully.

Make a paste (roux) with the flour and 1 heaped teaspoon butter. (Ideally, I'd prefer to remove the rabbit meat before thickening the sauce. If you don't feel up to this, just remember to be very careful while incorporating the roux so that you don't overcook the meat.) Bring the pan back to a fast simmer and slowly whisk in the paste in small amounts to thicken the mixture. Remove from the heat and allow to cool.

Make and chill the pastry as instructed. Roll out the chilled pastry, then line 6 small pie dishes, such as dariole moulds, leaving a lip, and cut lids to fit. Refrigerate the pastry cases and lids for 20 minutes. Divide the filling between the chilled pastry cases. Lightly mix the egg and milk, then brush this over the pastry lids. Position the lids egg-side down on the pies. Using a fork, press down around the edge of each pie to seal and trim away any excess pastry. Refrigerate the pies while heating the oven to 200°C.

Stand the pies on a baking tray and egg-wash the lids. Bake for 30–40 minutes until golden brown. Remove from the oven and allow to rest for 5 minutes before turning out. **Makes 6**

fillets   You can remove the fillets from the reserved saddles to make the Scaloppine of Rabbit with Sage, Wild Olives and Baked Radicchio on page 310.

Scaloppine of Rabbit with Sage, Wild Olives and Baked Radicchio

Years ago Madeleine Kamman, an American-based French food writer and teacher I admire greatly, had lunch at the Pheasant Farm. Madeleine didn't mince her words, and I was relieved to hear her say, 'Good! So few people can cook rabbit.' I tell this story to underline the point that rabbit is so frequently overcooked, and has a bad reputation as a result. Take note of the cooking times here.

8 rabbit fillets from 4 saddles

extra-virgin olive oil

freshly ground black pepper

28 sage leaves

4 radicchio hearts

90 g unbleached plain flour

sea salt

unsalted butter

$\frac{1}{2}$ cup pitted wild black *or* tiny Ligurian olives

$\frac{1}{4}$ cup verjuice

1 tablespoon jellied golden chicken stock

Preheat the oven to 200°C. Remove all sinew, if present, from the rabbit fillets, then smear the fillets with olive oil, grind on some pepper and scatter 8 of the sage leaves over them. Cover with plastic film and set aside.

Brush a baking dish with a little olive oil. Cut the radicchio hearts in half lengthwise, then pour over $\frac{1}{4}$ cup olive oil and bake for 15 minutes.

Remove the rabbit fillets from their plate and discard the sage. Cover the fillets with a doubled layer of plastic film and gently pound with a mallet until flattened to an even thickness. Season the flour with salt and pepper and lightly dust each fillet. Heat 30 g butter in a frying pan until nut-brown and foamy, then pan-fry the fillets gently for 2 minutes on each side. Remove the fillets from the pan and rest in a warm place.

Add a little more butter to the pan and fry the remaining sage leaves until crisp, then set aside. Toss the olives in the pan until warmed through, then set aside. Deglaze the pan with the verjuice and add the jellied stock. Simmer until slightly reduced in volume.

Serve 2 fillets per person and spoon over the sauce. Scatter the crisped sage leaves and olives over the rabbit and serve with the radicchio alongside. Serves 4

Ham in Hay

I've often drooled over the regional delicacies in Robert Freson's *The Taste of France*, and have always meant to cook this Lyonnaise dish. But my only guides were a photograph and a line that freshly mown hay is used. The timing was critical: a friend delivered the hay, cut just that week, the ham came from Schulz's (see pages 202–5), and the rest was instinct. It tastes as good as it looks.

1 leg of ham

1 kg freshly mown hay

3 large sprigs bay leaf

quince paste

verjuice

Put the leg of ham into a deep bucket and cover with cold water. Leave to soak for 24 hours.

Put half the hay into a deep stockpot, then put the ham on top and scatter over the bay leaves. Cover with the remaining hay. Cover with cold water and bring the pot to a boil – this can take up to 1½ hours. Turn down to a gentle simmer and cook for 2 hours.

Meanwhile, make a quince glaze by cooking 2 parts quince paste with 1 part verjuice until syrupy. The glaze should be sweet–sour and quite thick.

Preheat the upper element or grill in your oven to high. Remove the ham from the pot and clean it of any hay. Drain the cooking water from the hay. Cut a zigzag patterned 'collar' around the shin end of the leg and peel back the skin. Put the leg into a large baking tray and smear it with the quince glaze. Grill the in ham the oven, rotating it regularly to crisp the fat evenly. Serve on a bed of the reserved hay and bay leaves.

quince glaze   I make quince glaze commercially, if you don't feel like making your own.

The Dairy

My children were brought up on unpasteurised milk from Hilda Laurencis's dairy. Hilda, who has been part of our life since she came to work with us twenty-five years ago, was the first to show me what real milk and cream are about, and when she had excess cream we often made butter in the early days of the restaurant. (In case you're wondering, it's legal to sell unpasteurised milk and cream in South Australia; but you can't make cheese with it, more's the pity.)

After Hilda's dairy became a casualty of quotas, I found it impossible to be satisfied with commercial milk, and soon the Kernich family dairy at Greenock became our mainstay. The Kernichs, with three daughters and a son, have Jersey cows, and they are passionate about them. It's not difficult to see why: these doe-eyed cows are so handsome, with smooth skins in all shades of caramel, and they have very even temperaments. What makes Jerseys extra special is that their milk has a high fat content. While large companies actually penalise producers for this, I suggest you try custard or ice-cream made with Jersey milk and taste the difference.

When we had the restaurant, we'd pick up milk and cream several times a week. I bought a special stainless steel container with a lid that sat 5 cm down into it, so slurping milk was never a problem during transit. Sadly, I don't need the same quantities now as I did back then, but I still enjoy the chance to visit the dairy whenever I can.

There's something particularly engaging about the sweet, musty smell of a dairy, the cows waiting patiently in line, steam rising from their backs, and the way the animals nuzzle contentedly into their grain as they're milked. The rhythm of the whole process is mesmerising and satisfying (not forgetting plain hard and dirty work, however). I envy the dairy farmer who can fill a bucket with warm, frothy milk straight from the vat when the

house supplies run low. How every city child who thinks milk comes from cartons would delight in this.

Last time I visited the Kernichs, the cows were between seasons, but three had been kept in to milk. The Kernichs wanted to experiment with making cheese, and were kind enough to spare a bucket of milk for me as I wanted to make some curd as well as ice-cream. Geoff also separated cream for me to take home. It didn't look much different from the milk, in fact, but by next morning it was so thick that a spoon stood up in it! And how wonderful it tasted – it would have been easy to have eaten far more than would have been polite (or good for us) as we spread it over just-made scones with jam (pages 324–5).

The Kernich family have decided that the only way they can make the dairy viable for them all is to make the most of the milk of which they're all so proud by selling it direct to the public and by building a cheese factory on site. I couldn't be more delighted. Geoff says he got the idea years ago when Steve Flamsteed (a trained chef, winemaker and cheesemaker, friend and former employee) and I flirted with the idea of cheesemaking. It's so much more appropriate that the dairy farmer becomes the cheesemaker.

The cheese factory is being designed by the same architect we used for our Export Kitchen; meanwhile, the older daughters, Amy and Paula (Lisa is still at school), are already undertaking cheesemaking and quality-assurance courses. Paula came to our kitchen for work experience to get the feel of the hygiene requirements, too.

The day after my last visit I sent back as a thank-you some ice-cream I had made with honey from the Rosenzweigs (see pages 280–3) and that wonderful Jersey milk and cream, and wondered whether another idea might not be there for the taking.

White Bread

I can't count the number of times I've shared this recipe and was thought to have left out a secret ingredient – there's nothing secret about it, I just use really good flour. In fact, I have used nothing but the local Laucke flour since moving to the Barossa in 1973. Good flour is far from guaranteed, and good millers are rare, so check your source carefully – see further comments on page 322.

25 g fresh *or* 2½ teaspoons
  dried yeast

½ teaspoon castor sugar

warm water

1 kg unbleached strong flour

2 teaspoons sea salt

45 ml extra-virgin olive oil

Combine the yeast, castor sugar and warm water in a small bowl, then dissolve the yeast by mashing it with a fork and set aside for 5–10 minutes until frothy.

Combine the flour, salt and olive oil in the bowl of an electric mixer fitted with a dough hook, then add the yeast mixture. With the mixer set on a slow speed, gradually add 600 ml warm water to make a soft dough. Knead with the dough hook for 3 minutes, then turn the dough out onto a floured surface. Knead the dough by hand for a further 5 minutes, until it feels tight and the surface appears slightly broken.

Brush the mixing bowl with a little olive oil and return the dough. Roll the dough around the bowl to coat with the oil, then place a piece of plastic film loosely over the surface of the dough. Leave in a draught-free place until doubled in volume, 30–45 minutes.

Turn the dough out onto a floured surface again and knead it lightly for 2 minutes. Shape into 4 medium-sized loaves or 2 large, depending on the size of your bread tins (mine, as shown opposite, are very deep). Transfer the dough to the tins, then sprinkle with a little flour and leave in a draught-free place to rise a second time, 15–20 minutes, making sure you don't let the dough over-prove.

Meanwhile, preheat the oven to 220°C. Carefully put the loaves in the oven and bake for 10 minutes. Reduce the temperature to 180°C and bake for a further 20–25 minutes. Remove the tins from the oven and carefully tip out the bread. Put the loaves directly onto the oven racks and bake for a further 5 minutes to crisp the crust. Turn out onto a wire rack and allow to cool completely before cutting. Makes 2–4

plastic film   Sophie the bread witch taught me a great tip about covering rising dough with plastic film. Instead of covering the bowl, she lays a piece of plastic film loosely over the dough itself. The reason? If the dough has to push against plastic film that is stuck to the outside of the bowl, the rising process will be inhibited. Simple.

Walnut Bread

When making any bread with walnuts in it, never omit the step of roasting them, as these nuts are almost always rancid when sold shelled. This bread is particularly delicious with cheese – try the Fresh Goat's Curd with Walnut Oil, Rocket and Walnut Bread on page 276, where the bread is made into croutons.

125 g walnuts

15 g fresh *or* 1½ teaspoons
  dried yeast

½ teaspoon castor sugar

¼ cup warm water

milk

350 g unbleached strong flour

1 teaspoon sea salt

2 tablespoons walnut oil

150 ml sour cream

1 free-range egg

Preheat the oven to 220°C. Roast the walnuts on a baking tray for about 5 minutes, shaking the trays to prevent the nuts from burning. If they are not fresh season's, rub the walnuts in a clean tea towel to remove the bitter skins. Allow to cool.

Combine the yeast, castor sugar and warm water in a small bowl, then dissolve the yeast by mashing it with a fork and set aside for 5–10 minutes until frothy.

Meanwhile, warm 250 ml milk and set aside. Combine the flour, salt, walnut oil and walnuts in the bowl of an electric mixer fitted with a dough hook, then add the yeast mixture. Combine the warm milk and sour cream. With the mixer set on a slow speed, gradually mix the sour cream and milk into the flour to make a soft but not sloppy dough.

Turn the dough out onto a floured surface and knead it gently for 8 minutes. Brush the mixing bowl with a little more walnut oil and return the dough. Roll the dough around the bowl to coat with the oil, then place a piece of plastic film loosely over the surface of the dough. Leave in a draught-free place until doubled in volume, 30–45 minutes.

Turn the dough out onto a floured surface again and gently knead it for 2 minutes. Shape into 2 baguettes and leave to rise on a baking tray dusted with flour in a draught-free place for 10–15 minutes. Meanwhile, preheat the oven to 220°C. Mix the egg with 1 tablespoon milk and lightly brush this over the loaves. Bake for 10 minutes, then reduce the temperature to 180°C and bake for a further 15 minutes. Turn out onto a wire rack and allow to cool completely before cutting.

Makes 2 baguettes

flour   After trialling this bread with me in the Barossa, my friend and colleague Sophie Zalokar made it at home in Western Australia and found she needed an extra 150 g flour! The amount of flour needed in a recipe can vary simply because flour itself differs across brands and States. The harder the flour, the more liquid is required. Get used to how your dough feels and learn to mix in the flour carefully, adding or subtracting a little as necessary. Making the best bread requires the best-quality flour and the freshest of yeast. If you can't source locally milled flour, choose stone-ground, unbleached organic flour over mass-produced 'powder'.

Mustard Bread

I like to make crab sandwiches (page 294) with this bread. It's also fabulous toasted and spread with unsalted butter and leftover pot-roasted tongue (page 231), topped with a cornichon or two. Mustard bread freezes well, particularly if put into a freezer bag while still hot. The small loaves make great barbecue fare – crisp the defrosted bread in a hot oven and then split to take a grilled pork sausage.

⅓ cup burghul

¼ cup tepid water

25 g fresh *or* 2½ teaspoons
  dried yeast

½ teaspoon castor sugar

warm water

¼ cup grainy Dijon mustard

1 tablespoon maple syrup

1 tablespoon extra-virgin
  olive oil

340 g wholemeal strong flour

120 g unbleached strong flour

2 teaspoons salt

Soak the burghul in the ¼ cup tepid water until the water has been absorbed, about 20 minutes.

Combine the yeast, castor sugar and ¼ cup warm water in a small bowl, then dissolve the yeast by mashing it with a fork and set aside for 5–10 minutes until frothy.

Mix the mustard, maple syrup, olive oil and 250 ml warm water in a bowl. Combine the flours and salt in the bowl of an electric mixer fitted with a dough hook, then add the yeast mixture. With the mixer set on a slow speed, gradually add the mustard mixture to the flours to make a sticky, soft dough.

Turn the dough out onto a well-floured surface and knead it gently for 3–5 minutes. You will probably need to use quite a bit of extra flour to stop the dough sticking to the bench as the mixture will be tacky and soft.

Brush the mixing bowl with a little more olive oil and return the dough. Roll the dough around the bowl to coat with the oil, then place a piece of plastic film loosely over the surface of the dough. Leave in a draught-free place until doubled in volume, 45–60 minutes.

Turn the dough out onto a floured surface again and knead it gently for 2 minutes. Form the dough into 2 small loaves or 10–12 dariole-sized loaves. Transfer the dough to the tins or moulds and leave to rise in a draught-free place for 30 minutes. Meanwhile, preheat the oven to 220°C. Bake the larger loaves for 45 minutes and the smaller ones for 15–25 minutes. Turn out onto a wire rack and allow to cool completely before cutting. **Makes 2 small or 10–12 tiny loaves**

Scones

My mother made beautiful scones, but my own efforts have always been heavy as lead. The luscious cream we collected from the Kernichs' dairy, the help of my grandchildren and the presence of Sophie, once my apprentice and now my teacher, encouraged me to try again recently. Success! Thanks, Sophie – these scones are light as a feather (Mum would be proud).

450 g unbleached self-raising
  flour
1 pinch salt
1 tablespoon baking powder
1 tablespoon castor sugar
100 g chilled unsalted butter
milk

Preheat the oven to 220°C, making sure your oven racks are in position. Sift the flour, salt, baking powder and castor sugar into a bowl. Dice the chilled butter and rub into the flour quickly and gently with your fingertips, the coolest part of your hands, until the mixture resembles fine breadcrumbs. Make a well and pour in 320 ml milk. Using a fork, slowly combine the milk and flour until a soft dough forms. Don't handle the mixture more than you need.

Turn the dough out onto a floured surface and gently press it into a disc, then roll it out until 2.5–3 cm thick. Using a 4 cm round, straight-sided cutter, quickly cut shapes from the dough, rotating the cutter as you push down. (This screwing motion leaves the sides of the scones open, which allows for better rising.) Re-form the dough, then gently roll it out and cut more shapes.

Spread the scones out on a baking tray and brush the tops with a little milk. Bake for 20–25 minutes until risen and golden brown. Don't be tempted to open the oven door in the first 5 minutes or the scones will not rise properly. Cool for 5 minutes on a wire rack, then place the scones in a tea-towel-lined basket and cover with the corners of the towel. Eat immediately, or at worst within a couple of hours of cooking, with Strawberry Jam (page 266) and cream. **Makes 10–15**

sophie's tips I asked Sophie to let me in on her secret to making featherlight scones. 'I try to imagine how an old woman's hands look when making the dough, how she applies just the right amount of pressure when rubbing the butter into the flour, lifting and forking through the mixture with her fingers as she goes – nibble, light and swift, each action made in the same manner.' I remember my mother working exactly this way.

In addition to the above, Sophie's tips are that you should let the weight of the rolling pin do the work for you; you shouldn't push or boss the dough around too much. After cutting out the scones, screwing the cutter as you go as mentioned opposite, she warns that you must be careful that you don't let the milk slop over the sides of the scones when glazing them, as this will inhibit rising. Make sure your oven is hot – a hot oven shocks the dough into action – and bake the scones on the middle shelf, saving them from burnt bottoms or overly crusty tops. Opening the door, Sophie says, is suicide: the oven has to recover the temperature and in the meantime the scones have lost their thrust.

Good luck!

Olive Oil Dessert Cake with Poached Loquats

There is no doubt that Alice Waters' famous olive oil and sauternes cake was the initial inspiration for this, but more reading showed that olive oil has long been added to Italian cakes to give an incredibly moist finish. Loquats, one of the few fruits of spring, are so often ignored. Hating waste, I added their syrup to the cake – going with the flow is the story of all cooking.

12 loquats

2 vanilla beans

3 lemons

280 g castor sugar

¼ cup water

400 ml white wine

icing sugar

olive oil dessert cake

5 large free-range egg yolks

145 g castor sugar

finely grated zest of 5 lemons

125 ml syrup from the
  poached loquats

125 ml extra-virgin olive oil

150 g unbleached plain flour

1 pinch salt

3 free-range egg whites

1 pinch cream of tartar

Peel the loquats carefully and split the vanilla beans lengthwise with a small, sharp knife. Remove the zest from the lemons with a potato peeler and juice 2 of the lemons (you need about 160 ml juice). Bring the castor sugar and water to a boil and cook until amber-coloured. Standing well back, as the mixture will spit, add the wine, strips of lemon zest and vanilla beans. Bring to a gentle simmer, then add the loquats and poach until just tender. Add the lemon juice to the syrup to reduce the sweetness – taste the syrup as you go, adding a little juice at a time. Reserve 125 ml of the syrup for the cake.

To make the cake, preheat the oven to 180°C and grease and line a 22 cm springform cake tin. Beat the egg yolks with half the castor sugar and the finely grated lemon zest in an electric mixer until thick and pale. With the mixer on a slow speed, slowly add the reserved poaching syrup, then the olive oil. Sift the flour and salt over the mixture and beat until smooth.

In a clean bowl, beat the egg whites with the cream of tartar until soft peaks form. Slowly add the remaining castor sugar and continue to beat to make a thick, soft meringue. Take a spoonful of the meringue and fold it into the batter. Pour the batter into the meringue and fold until well incorporated. Spoon the batter into the prepared tin and bake for 20 minutes. Reduce the temperature to 160°C and bake for a further 20 minutes. Remove the cake from the oven and place a buttered disc of greaseproof paper over the top as it cools. This will stop the cake from drying out and allow it to cool slowly.

Dust with icing sugar and serve with the poached loquats and their syrup. **Serves 10–12**

traditional or otherwise   I use the poaching syrup from the loquats here instead of the dessert wine that appears in more traditional Italian versions of this cake. Another option would be to replace the poaching syrup with verjuice that has been reduced until golden and a little viscous and to use half the amount of zest in the syrup. This would make the cake a little lighter in colour and texture.

Charlick's Pavlovas

We had these pavlovas on the menu at Charlick's for two years running, they were so popular. They were made large enough to be almost obscene, but their generous size meant fewer disasters when making enough to fill an industrial oven. The trick is to make sure that the inside stays gooey, while the outside is crunchy.

3 large free-range egg whites

220 g castor sugar

1½ teaspoons cornflour

1 teaspoon white-wine vinegar

½ teaspoon pure vanilla

  extract

Preheat the oven to 150°C. Grease 2 large baking trays and line them with baking paper. Whisk the egg whites until soft peaks form. Gradually beat in the castor sugar and continue to beat until the meringue is stiff. Fold in the cornflour, then the vinegar and vanilla extract.

Mound the meringue into 4–6 thick small 'nests', making the edges slightly higher than the centre. Bake for 30 minutes, then turn off the oven and leave the pavlovas in it for a further 30 minutes before taking them out to cool on a wire rack.

Fill with cream and whatever you feel like – I can never go past sliced ladyfinger bananas and passionfruit. **Serves 4–6**

Sophie's Peach and Ginger Sandwiches

At the end of their four years (and they all stayed for that and more), my apprentices at the Pheasant Farm were 'given' a night of their own. They planned the menu, were in command of the kitchen, chose the music and invited the guests (who all paid, so the pressure was on). At the end of the meal, the apprentice had to address the gathering. This was Sophie's 'graduation' dessert.

4–6 ripe free-stone yellow
 peaches

1 litre best-quality vanilla
 ice-cream

ginger cake

80 g Buderim honeyed
 (candied) ginger

180 g softened unsalted butter

180 g castor sugar

3 × 61 g free-range eggs

¼ cup finely minced ginger

1 teaspoon finely grated
 lemon zest

325 g unbleached plain flour

1½ teaspoons baking powder

2 pinches ground mace

2 pinches salt

¼ cup milk

Preheat the oven to 200°C and grease a medium loaf tin. To make the ginger cake, finely chop the candied ginger. Cream the butter and castor sugar in an electric mixer until pale and thick. Add the eggs one at a time, beating well between each addition. Add the fresh and candied ginger and the lemon zest and mix well. Sift in the flour, baking powder, mace and salt and, while incorporating these, slowly pour in the milk. Spoon the batter into the prepared tin and bake for 30–40 minutes. Turn out onto a wire rack to cool.

Slice and stone the peaches. When ready to serve, layer slices of the cake with spoonfuls of vanilla ice-cream and slices of peach. **Serves 8**

Yellow Peach Tart with Bitter-almond Ice-cream

Scrumptious and oh-so-simple. The success of this tart relies on the pastry base being well cooked and the griller being really hot, so the peaches caramelise rather than stew. The edges of the pastry will appear burnt after this, but they add to the contrast between the sweet, juicy peaches and the crisp and caramelised sugar and pastry.

1 quantity Sour Cream Pastry
 (page 127)
9 ripe yellow free-stone peaches
50 g softened unsalted butter
¼ cup demerara sugar

bitter-almond ice-cream

50 g almonds
600 ml milk
400 ml cream
⅛ teaspoon bitter-almond
 extract
10 free-range egg yolks
110 g castor sugar

Preheat the oven to 220°C. To make the ice-cream, roast the almonds on a baking tray for about 5 minutes, shaking the tray to prevent the nuts from burning. Allow to cool. Grind the cooled nuts finely in a food processor. Bring the milk, cream, bitter-almond extract and ground almonds to a boil in a saucepan. Turn off the heat and leave for a minimum of 1 hour for the flavours to infuse.

Whisk the egg yolks with the castor sugar. Heat the infused milk and whisk it into the yolks. Return the custard to the saucepan and stir vigorously with a wooden spoon over a very low heat until the custard has cooked enough to coat the back of the spoon. Strain through a fine sieve and allow to cool before refrigerating. Churn the chilled custard in an ice-cream machine according to the manufacturer's instructions.

To make the peach tart, make and chill the pastry as instructed. Roll it out into a large rectangle about 3 mm thick. Lightly prick the pastry with a fork and refrigerate for 20 minutes. Meanwhile, preheat the oven to 200°C. Bake the pastry sheet in the oven until golden brown, about 20 minutes.

Preheat a griller to high. Peel and cut the peaches into large chunks and arrange on the sheet of baked pastry, butting the chunks up close to one another. Dot the butter over the peaches and sprinkle evenly with the demerara sugar. Stand the tart under the grill, rotating the tray to caramelise the peaches evenly – the pastry will almost burn, providing a contrast to the sweet fruit. Serve straight from the oven with a dollop of bitter-almond ice-cream. Serves 8–10

bitter almonds   If you are lucky enough to have access to bitter almonds, omit the extract, and replace 3–4 regular almonds with the bitter ones. (Remember that bitter almonds are poisonous if eaten in large quantities.) Many almond growers have a bitter-almond tree in their orchard (I do), sometimes just because it's a throwback. If you know an Italian family with one, you'll find they keep the nuts separate and revere them.

Lavender-and-honey Ice-cream

On the same 1986 trip that Madeleine Kamman visited the Pheasant Farm (see page 310), I assisted her in the first-ever cooking demonstration held at the Yalumba Winery near Angaston, where she made an ice-cream that inspired this one. Mine is a simpler version – hers included orange, roasted almonds, dried thyme and more cream and egg yolks.

600 ml milk

400 ml cream

1 pinch salt

6 large French-lavender heads

10 free-range egg yolks

⅔ cup single-variety honey

Bring the milk, cream and salt to a boil in a saucepan with the lavender heads. Turn off the heat and leave for a minimum of 1 hour for the flavours to infuse. Taste the infusion – the lavender flavour needs to be very strong if it's to survive being frozen, which dulls the flavour. If necessary, reheat the milk and infuse with more lavender.

In a mixing bowl, whisk the egg yolks with the honey. Heat the infused milk and whisk it into the yolks. Return the custard to the saucepan and stir vigorously with a wooden spoon over a very low heat until the custard is thick enough to coat the back of the spoon. Strain it through a fine sieve and allow to cool before refrigerating. Churn the chilled custard in an ice-cream machine according to the manufacturer's instructions. As with all homemade ice-cream, the flavour is best the day it is made. Serves 8–10

honey   The flavour of honey diminishes with age. It is most fragrant when first collected, making spring the time for this dish.

Cold Lemon Soufflé

We made this simple dessert at the Pheasant Farm in large quantities, and served scoops as it was ordered. When eating with friends in France's Dordogne not long ago, we had a similar dessert; this time, a large communal bowl was brought to the table for us to help ourselves. This gesture showed such flair and generosity, and while no one kept tabs on us, none of us abused the privilege.

3 × 61 g free-range eggs

3 lemons

100 g castor sugar

2 gelatine leaves

¼ cup hot water

300 ml rich cream (45% fat)

Separate the eggs. Finely grate the zest of the lemons and then juice them (you need 100 ml strained juice). Bring a large saucepan of water to a boil. Put the egg yolks, zest, juice and castor sugar into a large stainless steel bowl and set this over the boiling water, then whisk until pale and thick. Remove the bowl and set it aside.

Soften the gelatine in a little cold water for 5 minutes, then squeeze out any excess moisture and dissolve the leaves in the hot water. Whisk this into the egg mixture and refrigerate until cold and just starting to set. Whisk the cream until soft peaks form, then fold this through the cold sabayon. Refrigerate until just starting to set. Whisk the egg whites until soft peaks form (be careful not to overwhip them or the texture of the final dessert will be crumbly rather than soft and light) and fold these through too. Spoon the mixture into individual dishes or a large bowl and refrigerate until set, about 3 hours. Serves 6

Hazelnut Meringue with Raspberries and Hazelnut Butter Cream

A truly decadent and very tactile dessert. The meringue becomes the platter on which the irresistible hazelnut butter cream is served. The raspberries, which can be piled on top or layered throughout, add a freshness to the fabulously gooey mass. I have delighted in using raspberries any way I can since they began being farmed near Mt McKenzie on the edge of the Barossa.

1 punnet raspberries
icing sugar

hazelnut meringue
250 g hazelnuts
castor sugar
1 tablespoon unbleached
  plain flour
9 × 61 g free-range egg whites
1 pinch salt

hazelnut butter cream
100 g hazelnuts
100 g castor sugar
90 ml water
2 large free-range egg yolks
115 g softened unsalted
  butter

Preheat the oven to 200°C. Put the hazelnuts for both the meringue and the butter cream onto a baking tray and roast for about 5 minutes, shaking the tray to prevent the nuts from burning. Rub the hazelnuts in a clean tea towel to remove the skins, then transfer the nuts to a coarse sieve to remove any remaining skin. Allow to cool. Reduce the oven temperature to 140°C.

To make the meringue, line 3 baking trays with baking paper and draw a 20 cm circle in the middle of each one. Finely grind 250 g of the roasted hazelnuts in a food processor with 300 g castor sugar and the flour until the mixture resembles fine breadcrumbs. In the bowl of an electric mixer, whisk the egg whites with the salt until soft peaks form, then add 1 tablespoon castor sugar to stabilise the mixture. Continue whisking until the meringue is stiff. Fold in the nut mixture and divide the meringue between the 3 circles on the baking paper, smoothing the top of each disc. Bake for 1 hour, then turn off the oven, leaving the meringues in it to cool.

To make the hazelnut butter cream, finely grind the remaining roasted hazelnuts in a food processor and set aside. Put 50 g of the castor sugar and 1 tablespoon of the water into a saucepan and stand it over a high heat. Allow to boil until a golden caramel colour. Standing well back, as the caramel will spit, pour in the remaining water and cook for a further 2 minutes. Remove from the heat. Whisk the egg yolks and remaining castor sugar in an electric mixer until pale and thick. With the mixer set on a slow speed, slowly pour in the hot caramel, continuing to beat until the mixture is thick and cool. Slowly add knobs of the softened butter until well incorporated, then mix in the ground hazelnuts.

To assemble, put a meringue disc on a flat plate and spread it with a third of the hazelnut butter cream. Repeat with the remaining meringues and butter cream, then pile fresh raspberries over the final layer of butter cream and dust with a little icing sugar before serving. Serves 8–10

Quandong Trifle

Trifle has 'country' written all over it. And the addition of quandongs, a great Australian flavour, makes this even more special. I've reconstituted dried quandongs in verjuice to emphasise their piquant flavour – this fruit is brilliant to work with and I wish it wasn't so fragile to produce. Serve the trifle in your best glass or crystal bowl at the table, just as your grandmother would have done.

2½ cups dried quandongs

500 ml verjuice

¼ cup slivered almonds

250 g castor sugar

115 ml flor fino sherry

500 ml double cream

sponge

3 × 55 g free-range eggs

60 g unsalted butter

unbleached plain flour

85 g castor sugar

65 g cornflour

1 teaspoon cream of tartar

½ teaspoon bicarbonate
  of soda

brandy custard

¼ cup brandy

1 vanilla bean

300 ml milk

300 ml cream

8 free-range egg yolks

75 g castor sugar

Soak the quandongs in the verjuice overnight. Next day, preheat the oven to 220°C. Roast the almonds on a baking tray for about 5 minutes, shaking the tray to prevent the nuts from burning. Allow to cool. Reduce the oven temperature to 180°C.

To make the sponge, immerse the eggs in a little warm water for 10 minutes. Melt 20 g of the butter and grease a 23 cm square cake tin. Dust the tin evenly with a little plain flour and shake out any excess. Whisk the eggs with the castor sugar in an electric mixer until pale and thick. Sift the cornflour, cream of tartar, bicarbonate of soda and 1 tablespoon plain flour into the creamed mixture, then, using a hand whisk, fold in gently. Melt the remaining butter and pour it into the batter, then fold in until incorporated. Pour the batter into the prepared cake tin and bake for 20–25 minutes, until lightly coloured. If cooked, the cake should spring back when touched lightly. Leave the cake in the tin for 5 minutes, then turn it out onto a wire rack to cool.

To make the custard, put the brandy into a non-reactive saucepan, then slit the vanilla bean and scrape the seeds into the brandy. Simmer gently for 1 minute. Heat the milk and cream in another non-reactive saucepan and add the brandy infusion. Whisk the egg yolks and castor sugar, then slowly whisk in the hot brandy milk. Return the saucepan to the stove and stir vigorously over a very low heat until the custard is thick and coats the back of a spoon. Strain through a fine sieve and allow to cool. Refrigerate until well chilled, with plastic film pressed down onto the surface of the custard to prevent a skin from forming.

Drain the quandongs and reserve their soaking liquid – you should have at least 250 ml. Put the soaking liquid, castor sugar and all but 1 tablespoon sherry into a non-reactive saucepan and bring to a boil. Simmer gently for 5 minutes, until the syrup thickens slightly, then add the quandongs. Simmer for a further 5 minutes or until the quandongs are cooked right through but are still intact, then allow to cool before refrigerating.

To put the trifle together, cut the sponge into 1.5 cm cubes and scatter over the base of your chosen dish. Drizzle the remaining sherry and enough of the quandong syrup over the sponge to moisten it thoroughly. Dot a few quandongs over the sponge, then pour in a good layer of custard. Allow the custard to seep into and through the sponge layer before spooning in the cream. Smooth the top and dot the remaining quandongs over the cream. Scatter on the toasted almond slivers and serve. If prepared in advance, refrigerate the trifle but allow it to return to room temperature before serving as the flavours will be bolder and the texture more luscious. Serves 6–8

tips   If your double cream is not thick, you can use 500 ml 45% fat cream, whipped until soft peaks form. The extra tablespoon of sherry adds a traditional alcoholic note to the trifle, but the dish will not suffer if it is omitted. All the components can be made the day before.

Acknowledgements

While this book has my name on it, the involvement of a great number of other people ensured its eventual completion. There would never have been a book in the first place without Julie Gibbs, my friend and publisher; she makes things happen, pushing and cajoling when necessary, but all the time nurturing. She really understands me, which makes working with her on each book a new and wonderful journey. And she has the best eye you could ever imagine – she even took time out of her frenetic schedule to fossick through the kitchen and Col's shed to pull together treasures for the various photo shoots.

I am so lucky to have worked again with Simon Griffiths, a frequent visitor over the last year and with whom Colin and I have worked and holidayed in recent times. He and his camera have made my life spring so completely off these pages that even I have seen it all in a new light. Simon has done the Barossa proud, and I think his work is truly extraordinary.

My editor, Caroline Pizzey, I once wrote, has 'become my second skin', and I don't know how to improve on that. Ours is such a close relationship – she knows what's missing because she shares the same passion for food and the country as I do. I can't ever imagine writing without her – she is my combined sounding board and conscience. And then there's Katie Purvis, Senior Editor at Penguin, who oversaw the whole project in-house – in tandem with Production Controller Carmen De La Rue – and who was always encouraging and accommodating, giving important feedback in times of stress and doubt. The designer, Sandy Cull, became immersed in the project, and having assisted during the shoots, really came to grips with what we are all about. It's an interesting process having someone represent your sense of style on paper, and I think the simple beauty of her design absolutely sings.

One of the real reasons this book came into being was the involvement of the very special Sophie Zalokar. Sophie was one of my first apprentices at the Pheasant Farm Restaurant and now lives in Fremantle, Western Australia. Three times during the life of this project she left her husband, Chris, and two preschool children to be my assistant, my baker of bread, my sanity check, my friend. I may have taught her once, but she continually teaches me. Her passion for and talent with food is a very real part of the strength of this book and I couldn't have finished the project without her.

Nor would I have ever been free enough to take on this project without the support of my staff: Trevor Cook, the treasure of all times, head of production at the Export Kitchen; Clare Bogan, my friend and right-hand aid in so many things; Jane Renner, who has transformed and leads the Farm Shop; and the incredibly dedicated teams at both the Export Kitchen and Farm Shop. Every time there was a photo shoot, all my staff became involved in some way or another and helped make it happen. Thank you.

A special thank-you must go to my daughter Saskia, who jumped into the fray when needed and who, with her husband, Greg Price, provided their Barossa Farm Produce – chooks, milk-fed lamb, goose and turkey. There was also a band of people outside the Valley who responded to my frantic calls for produce. John O'Donnell, of Stall 69 at Adelaide Central Markets, became so involved in these requests that he even raided his mother's and friends' gardens on occasions, and delivered vegetables wrapped in damp tea towels to keep them fresh. Rev Cant from the Riverland supplied boxes of the most perfect citrus; Jim Mendolia from Fremantle provided me with sardines against all odds, and Perth's Vince Garreffa, from Mondo di Carne, sourced beautiful rabbits. When word went out we needed more plates for the final photo shoot, Julie's friend Ellen Cameron, from Blackheath Antiques in the Blue Mountains, kindly entrusted her treasures to an aeroplane to help out.

The photo shoots spanned more than a year, running with the seasons to catch every angle of the Valley. A huge vote of thanks must go to the locals who allowed their space to be turned upside down for Simon's lens: Rockford, for the basket-press crush; the Kernich family, for sharing their dairy (and cream and milk); Gloria and Mark Rosenzweig, for taming the bees; and the boys at Apex Bakery and Schulz's Butchers, for being accommodating, as ever. When the idea for this book was first mooted, the biennial Barossa Vintage Festival was in full swing and knowing we wouldn't have another chance to shoot the scarecrows that appear at this time each year, I asked Eric Algra to photograph them for me – the wonderful results can be seen on pages 60–1.

The pastry recipe on page 85 is reproduced by kind permission of *Australian Gourmet Traveller*. Jacques Pepin's words on page 145 are used by permission of Black Dog & Leventhal Publishers.

Part of the beauty of living in the Valley is knowing you can call on your network whenever there's a problem, as I did when I needed extra bits and pieces for photo shoots. Whether it was a beautiful plate, a family heirloom or a treasured something from a clearing sale, friend after friend, including Lorraine Ashmead, Jenny Beckmann, Wilma McLean, Liz Mosey, Sherri Schubert and Di Wark, came to the rescue in their special way. Their generosity is the hallmark of life here in the Barossa.

Finally, my husband, Colin, and daughters, Saskia and Ellie, and even our grandchildren, Zöe, Max and Lily, wondered at various times when it would all end, and when their wife, mother and nonna would have her life back – as did I at times. The richness of my existence in the Barossa stems from my life with Col, and I know well the strength of his love and support that allows me the freedom to be driven by this passionate but obsessive world of food. He is the centre of our family, and is always there for our daughters and grandchildren. I have been lucky in so many ways.

Bibliography

Alexander, Stephanie. *The Cook's Companion*, Viking, Ringwood, 1996.
—— *Stephanie's Australia*. Allen & Unwin, Sydney, 1991.
—— *Stephanie's Menus for Food Lovers*. Methuen Haynes, Sydney, 1985.
—— *Stephanie's Seasons*. Allen & Unwin, Sydney, 1993.
Alexander, Stephanie & Beer, Maggie. *Stephanie Alexander & Maggie Beer's Tuscan Cookbook*. Viking, Ringwood, 1998.
The Barossa Cookery Book. Soldiers' Memorial Institute, Tanunda, 1917.
Beck, Simone. *Simca's Cuisine*. Vintage, New York, 1976.
Beck, Simone, Bertholle, Louisette, & Child, Julia. *Mastering the Art of French Cooking* (vol.1). Penguin, Harmondsworth, 1966.
Beer, Maggie. *Cooking with Verjuice*. Viking, Ringwood, 2001.
—— *Maggie's Farm*. Allen & Unwin, Sydney, 1993.
—— *Maggie's Orchard*. Viking, Ringwood, 1997.
Bertolli, Paul with Waters, Alice. *Chez Panisse Cooking*. Random House, New York, 1988.
Boddy, Michael & Boddy, Janet. *Kitchen Talk* magazine. Bugle Press, via Binalong, NSW.
Boni, Ada. *Italian Regional Cooking*. Bonanza, New York, n.d.
Bureau of Resource Sciences. *Marketing Names for Fish and Seafood in Australia*. Department of Primary Industries & Energy and the Fisheries Research & Development Corporation, Canberra, 1995.
Castelvetro, Giacomo. *The Fruit, Herbs and Vegetables of Italy*. Viking, New York, 1990.
David, Elizabeth. *English Bread and Yeast Cookery*. Penguin, Harmondsworth, 1979.
—— *French Provincial Cooking*. Penguin, Harmondsworth, 1970.
—— *Italian Food*. Penguin, Harmondsworth, 1989.
—— *An Omelette and a Glass of Wine*. J.M. Dent, Melbourne, 1984.
De Groot, Roy. *Auberge of the Flowering Heart*. Ecco Press, New Jersey, 1973.
Freson, Robert. *The Taste of France*. Webb & Bower, Great Britain, 1983.
Grigson, Jane. *Charcuterie and French Pork Cookery*. Penguin, Harmondsworth, 1970.
—— *Jane Grigson's Fish Cookery*. Penguin, Harmondsworth, 1973.
—— *Jane Grigson's Fruit Book*. Michael Joseph, London, 1982.
—— *Jane Grigson's Vegetable Book*. Penguin, Harmondsworth, 1980.
Ioannou, Noris. *Barossa Journeys: Into a Valley of Tradition*. New Holland, Sydney, 2000.
Kamman, Madeleine. *In Madeleine's Kitchen*. Macmillan, New York, 1992.
—— *The Making of a Cook*. Atheneum, New York, 1978.
Malouf, Greg & Malouf, Lucy. *Arabesque*. Hardie Grant, Melbourne, 1999.
Manfield, Christine. *Paramount Cooking*. Viking, Ringwood, 1995.
McGee, Harold. *On Food and Cooking*. Collier, New York, 1988.
Olney, Richard. *Simple French Food*. Atheneum, New York, 1980.
Peck, Paula. *The Art of Fine Baking*. Simon & Schuster, New York, 1961.
Pellegrini, Angelo M. *The Food Lover's Garden*. Lyons & Burford, New York, 1970.
Pepin, Jacques. *La Technique*. Hamlyn, New York, 1978.
Ripe, Cherry. *Goodbye Culinary Cringe*. Allen & Unwin, Sydney, 1993.
Santich, Barbara. 'The return of verjuice', from *Winestate*, June 1984.
The Schauer Australian Cookery Book (14th edn). W.R. Smith & Paterson, Brisbane, 1979.
Scicolone, Michele. *The Antipasto Table*. Morrow, New York, 1991.
Scott, Philippa. *Gourmet Game*. Simon & Schuster, New York, 1989.
Simeti, Mary Taylor. *Pomp and Sustenance*. Alfred A. Knopf, New York, 1989.
Studd, Will. *Chalk and Cheese*. Purple Egg, Melbourne, 1999.
Symons, Michael. *One Continuous Picnic*. Duck Press, Adelaide, 1982.
Taruschio, Ann & Taruschio, Franco. *Leaves for the Walnut Tree*. Pavilion, London, 1993.
Waters, Alice. *The Chez Panisse Menu Cookbook*. Chatto & Windus, London, 1984.
Wells, Patricia. *At Home in Provence*. Scribner, New York, 1996.
Wells, Patricia & Robuchon, Joel. *Simply French*. Morrow, New York, 1991.
Wolfert, Paula. *Cooking of South West France*. Dial Press, New York, 1983.
— *The Cooking of the Eastern Mediterranean*. HarperCollins, New York, 1994.
— *Mediterranean Cooking*. Ecco Press, New York, 1977.

Index